Priesthood & Prophecy
Adonijah O. Ogbonnaya, Ph. D.

Publications Copyright © 2023, literature arm of AACTEV8 International
Edited by Kathy Strecker
Cover design - Edward Johnson of Elev8shin Inc
(Apostolic Activation Network)
Aactev8 International1020 Victoria Ave. Venice, CA 90291
www.aactev8.com

Published by Seraph Creative

Library of Congress data
Scripture quotations from the New American Standard Bible unless otherwise stated. NASB, KJV.

1

THE BINDING CONNECTION BETWEEN PRIESTHOOD AND PROPHECY

When the lamb was slain before
the foundation, it was not the
destruction of life but rather the
release of life into creation.

We need to talk about priesthood and prophecy. We have a misunderstanding of what our role is on the earth. It is easy to go into a camp that is not really what God wants us to do. To understand our role, especially in this particular time and age, we must learn about sonship, priesthood and prophecy. Sonship and priesthood are eternal. Prophecy is temporal. Priesthood always outlasts the prophetic because priesthood and sonship existed before the world was created. The whole process of prophecy is temporal because it occurs within creation. This scripture says:

> **Love never ends. As for prophecies, they will pass away; as for
> tongues, they will cease; as for knowledge, it will pass away.
> For we know in part and we prophesy in part, but when the
> perfect comes, the partial will pass away.
> (1 Corinthians 13:8-9)**

The structure of the prophetic and its effectiveness is grounded on how you view yourself both as a son and as a priest. As a matter of fact, Priesthood existed before the world was created. We know this because the Bible tells us about the lamb that was slain before the creation of the world:

...and all who dwell on earth will worship it, everyone whose name has not been written before the foundation of the world in the book of life of the Lamb who was slain.
(Revelation 13:8)

When the lamb was slain before the foundation, it was not the destruction of life but rather the release of life into creation. In other words, what God did before the creation of the world is foundational to the structure of the universe and how it carries itself.

Sonship was in God. It is the original principle of Divinity. The Divine begetting principle is foundational within the Divine. The very structure of this progenation is the production of someone who is the manifestation of God who cannot be seen. Sonship is grounded in Divinity. It is connected to intrinsic righteousness because it carries the nature of the begetters. That means that sonship carries God Himself into creation. A son carries the fullness of God: His righteousness, holiness, goodness, mercy and grace. If one is a son of God, that person carries, if not in manifestation, the potential of who God is. Being a child of God and begetting a son of God is fundamental to Divinity, which means that you and I who are born of God carry the fullness of God. Sonship grows into redemption, rectification, and healing. Sonship carries the fullness of Divinity within that which is begotten. Anyone born of God carries completely what God is.

You cannot be a priest if you are not the child of someone who operates at an altar. Not to be gender-cruel, but the Bible uses the term "son." The son becomes the priest in scripture. Priesthood, however, is originally a female function. Remember that Jacob had thirteen children. One of them was a woman named Dinah. After Israel is framed as a nation, Dinah is not mentioned. In addition, Jacob adopted one son of Joseph and moved one of his own sons, Levi, into the priesthood, which should have been the function of Dinah.

Priesthood is a position of the upper life or higher self of Israel where God needs humans for certain activities. How the priesthood was taken over by males, although it was originally a female function, is a rabbinical secret of secrets. The priest is the one who opens the gateways between this dimension and the other dimensions. In other words, they are keepers of the womb.

We have to start thinking in the context of this new era. What are the feminine functions that are needed to truly heal the world? Everything that human beings do even in their fallenness usually presages what God originally intended. All the issues we see today about gender, for example, are really about our human desire to return to what God intended where there is neither male nor female. In our fallen nature, we pursue this incorrectly from a purely physical perspective, yet it is ultimately a spiritual principle. Remember that, in Christ, we are one:

For as many of you as were baptized into Christ have put on Christ. There is neither Jew nor Greek, there is neither slave nor free, there is no male and female, for you are all one in Christ Jesus. (Galatians 3:27-28)

Therefore, the binary principle becomes one when we get into Christ, which means it can begin to produce.

Let us come back to the priesthood. In Israel, there are three types of priesthood. Every priest, unless they are initiated by adoption, carries the blood of the line of their priesthood. Priests will prophesy both according to the line that they carry and according to the function that they have within the priesthood. Sometimes the function of the priesthood is determined by certain things. The prophetic movement of your being is determined by how you function within your priesthood. If your function as a priest is flawed, then your prophecy will be flawed. If you do not understand yourself as a priest, you will end up prophesying from a position that causes you to misunderstand things and create more misunderstandings. We must, therefore, find out more about these three types of priesthood and what they mean for prophecy.

Remember, you are a son and, as a son, you are a priest as well. Priesthood has a strong feminine vibration and perspective. We know that most cultures have men as priests, but many old cultures have women as priests called priestesses. Because of the way that religion has functioned throughout history, the reality of the femininity of the priesthood was subjugated to the male principle in such a way that you had the males ministering at the altar of the womb of creation. This is not pagan—it is a reality. The temple is even built as a womb. You move from the outer across three dimensions into the Holy of Holies. The whole process within the temple is about going back into the womb of creation, into the depths of who God is, and coming back, being born completely anew through the doorways and the uterus of the temple.

Biology is a metaphor for theology. Your body is a temple of the Holy Spirit (1 Corinthians 6:19). How the temple in Israel was built aligns with how your body was built. In fact, the temple was built to mimic your body to reflect humanity in full.

Let us look at some scriptures that talk about the three types of priesthood and its different functions:

> On the outside of the inner gateway there were two chambers
> in the inner court, one at the side of the north gate facing
> south, the other at the side of the south gate facing north. And
> he said to me, "This chamber that faces south is for the priests
> who have charge of the temple, and the chamber that faces
> north is for the priests who have charge of the altar. These
> are the sons of Zadok, who alone among the sons of Levi may
> come near to the LORD to minister to him." (Ezekiel 40:44-46)

AND

> "Thus says the Lord GOD: No foreigner, uncircumcised in
> heart and flesh, of all the foreigners who are among the people
> of Israel, shall enter my sanctuary. But the Levites who went
> far from me, going astray from me after their idols when
> Israel went astray, shall bear their punishment. They shall be
> ministers in my sanctuary, having oversight at the gates of the
> temple and ministering in the temple. They shall slaughter the
> burnt offering and the sacrifice for the people, and they shall
> stand before the people, to minister to them. Because they
> ministered to them before their idols and became a stumbling
> block of iniquity to the house of Israel, therefore I have sworn
> concerning them, declares the Lord GOD, and they shall bear
> their punishment. They shall not come near to me, to serve
> me as priest, nor come near any of my holy things and the
> things that are most holy, but they shall bear their shame and
> the abominations that they have committed. Yet I will appoint
> them to keep charge of the temple, to do all its service and all
> that is to be done in it."

> But the Levitical priests, the sons of Zadok, who kept the
> charge of my sanctuary when the people of Israel went
> astray from me, shall come near to me to minister to me.
> And they shall stand before me to offer me the fat and the

blood, declares the Lord GOD. They shall enter my sanctuary, and they shall approach my table, to minister to me, and they shall keep my charge. When they enter the gates of the inner court, they shall wear linen garments. They shall have nothing of wool on them, while they minister at the gates of the inner court, and within. They shall have linen turbans on their heads, and linen undergarments around their waists. They shall not bind themselves with anything that causes sweat. And when they go out into the outer court to the people, they shall put off the garments in which they have been ministering and lay them in the holy chambers. And they shall put on other garments, lest they transmit holiness to the people with their garments. They shall not shave their heads or let their locks grow long; they shall surely trim the hair of their heads. No priest shall drink wine when he enters the inner court. They shall not marry a widow or a divorced woman, but only virgins of the offspring of the house of Israel, or a widow who is the widow of a priest. They shall teach my people the difference between the holy and the common, and show them how to distinguish between the unclean and the clean. In a dispute, they shall act as judges, and they shall judge it according to my judgments. They shall keep my laws and my statutes in all my appointed feasts, and they shall keep my Sabbaths holy. They shall not defile themselves by going near to a dead person. However, for father or mother, for son or daughter, for brother or unmarried sister they may defile themselves. After he has become clean, they shall count seven days for him. And on the day that he goes into the Holy Place, into the inner court, to minister in the Holy Place, he shall offer his sin offering, declares the Lord GOD. This shall be their inheritance: I am their inheritance: and you shall give them no possession in Israel; I am their possession. (Ezekiel 44:9-28)

There are four levels of priests with different functions. First is the high priest. The family of Aaron was chosen to be a priestly family. The high priests of God were chosen from Aaron's family to minister to God in the temple. This was how it was set up from the beginning. You had a priest, Moses, who was not supposed to be a priest. Moses ordained Aaron to be a priest. The next one is the sons of Levi who were also priests but did not minister inside the temple. Then you had all of Israel who were priests but who functioned outside. Within the very context of the prophets who ministered in the temple, you have the high priest, you have the people who made the sacrifice, and you have the people who took care of the victuals of the temple. In that time and place, it was meant that way because when you are put in that position of a priest and you know what your priestly function is, it affects the way you prophesy. By the time we come to the book of Ezekiel historically, God announces that the way we function in our priesthood affects the way we do ministry and the way we prophesy. It is in the context of the text.

When you read the Bible, you never hear that the High Priest ever uttered a prophecy, but the High Priest was a prophetic figure. Everything he did was prophetic. So, here is the problem. When your priesthood functions by ministering to people, your prophecy will then be about people. We find this in the account of Aaron and the golden calf. It was a prophecy that became about idolatry and destruction because it was focused on giving the people what they want and not ministering to God. What we see here demonstrates why prophecies go awry: because priests focus their minds on ministering to the people. They build the people's idols through the structure of Divinity and then the people run around and begin to worship other gods. So what happened? Exodus 32:1 says,

When the people saw that Moses delayed to come down from the mountain, the people gathered themselves together to Aaron and said to him, "Up, make us gods who shall go before us. As for this Moses, the man who brought us up out of the land of Egypt, we do not know what has become of him."

At this point, Aaron had not yet been fully initiated into his high-priestly role and was still functioning as a priest. He allowed the people to lead him to make an idol for them. It came out of the people's spirit of dissatisfaction and their desire to repeat what happened in Egypt and to return to the gods they knew in Egypt. Therefore, Aaron made a god, the golden calf. Then he began to worship it and pray, which led to Moses being kicked out of the presence of God. When Moses heard them celebrating, he knew it was not the fault of the prophet, but the fault of the priest. The priest had created a prophetic landscape so that the people were now prophesying from the spirit of an idol. When the priesthood goes awry, the prophecy becomes problematic. Prophecy is infected. Worship is infected. It becomes about entertainment and activity. The priest was the one who went along with the people and caused the problem. Remember, Moses was a Levite before he was a prophet. There is an intrinsic priesthood even in the prophetic movement of Moses. What made Moses' prophecy so powerful was that Moses was always prophesying from the perspective of ministering to God.

It is necessary for priests to minister to the people. That is not a problem. The problem is when the needs of the people become the determination for how the priest communicates Divinity to the people. This is a serious issue because it means that the people's mood swings, likes and dislikes, love and hate, and emotional ups and downs become the determinant for how the priest speaks. As a result, prophecy begins to be swayed by the mood swings of the people and the priest prophesies to the people by catering to what they think they need. This is what ministry has become—not the ministration to God but the ministration to people based on their changing whims. You see, if you prophesy to people from a direction that is different from their current mood, they get upset and when they get upset, they begin to leave. So, the priest prophesies in a way to try to keep them. If you do that, now your priesthood is informing your prophecy and your prophecy will get you stuck with people and their moods and you will no longer be able to read the mind of God accurately. The reason people cannot read the mind of God is because their whole focus is on making people feel good, which is not the same as making God feel good. Does this mean that ministering to people is not good? No.

Look again at what God says in Ezekiel 44. He says those priests who ministered to the people in their idols when they went astray, who went astray with them, and who ministered to them according to their need— those priests will bear their punishment. What is their punishment? It is to carry the burden of the people in such a way that it causes problems. One of the reasons that so many pastors die so early and from so many different types of diseases is because they are ministering to people in or according to their error, not from the perspective of God. You must not minister to people according to their own perspective, but rather from the perspective of Divinity. The moment you bend yourself towards meeting the immediate needs of the people according to their mood swings and emotional instability resulting from the vicissitudes of life, you end up carrying their burdens. You cannot carry all of that weight. Doing so affects your physical body, your soul, how you preach, and how you minister. And because humanity is so competitive, you cannot help but begin to minister in a competitive way as well. You want to be the one whom the people follow so you restructure your theology and how you speak. Then you begin to say things like, "Jesus Christ is not the only way," and you prophesy according to these compromises. When you act in this manner, you are not ministering to God or from His perspective but rather from the emotional instability of the people. Doing this then causes further instability and you end up causing even further confusion on the face of the earth.

You may help people in the near term, but it will create more problems in the long run because, if you only focus on "their needs," you never really allow the people to see God. The church has always taught leaders to focus on the needs of the people. How does that work? How many needs can you really focus on? You end up with a church full of emotionally immature people who traumatize each other in the name of trying to get your prophecy. Is your prophecy coming from the failure of your priesthood? Is your failed priesthood ultimately causing you to prophesy in a way that exaggerates their needs and afflictions, making it something cosmic and universal among the congregation or among all the people to whom you minister?

Now, remember, ministering to people is a good thing. When God established the priesthood, he allowed some of the priests to minister to the people and their ministration had various levels. A priest is vital. Priesthood is going to endure. In Revelation 1:6, the Bible says that God has made us kings and priests, not kings, priests, and prophets. Again, 1 Corinthians 13:8 tells us that prophecy shall cease. True prophecy must flow from sonship, kingship, and priesthood. When a prophecy does not flow from kingship and priesthood, it becomes a false prophecy because it is based on misperception and misdirection of the energy of priesthood. The people who minister to others must protect themselves from being influenced and directed by the emotional whims of the people.

The second type of priest is the one who ministers to the house. Do you remember that time in Pentecostalism when it was about building big buildings? It is a good thing—building the temple and ministering to the temple. But if you are not careful, ministering to things can lead you to prophesy about things and to things and for things. Again, how you tailor your priesthood affects the way you prophesy. Every believer has the capacity for prophecy, but their prophecy must flow from priesthood. What is a priest supposed to do so that their prophecy moves in a transformative direction and does not mislead people? What has happened in this context recently? Why did so many of us miss what God was saying in spite of the fact that it was so obvious what He was saying? I am not trying to be arrogant. I stayed quiet for a long time and I even went along with people who prophesied from that perspective until the Lord would not let me rest. When you look at current events, you realize that leaders are ministering to the people from the perspective of things and systems. So, if you are a priest and you latch yourself to a system because it provides you relevance, that system can end up affecting your capacity to prophesy.

Let me give you an example. We know of at least two Major Prophets in the Bible who were priests: Jeremiah and Ezekiel. Isaiah was a scribe for the king. Moses was also a priest. I believe Hosea was a priest. Zechariah was a priest. They understood priesthood and they prophesied according to their focus and what they served. Ministering to things is okay because people need things. On the other hand, ministering to people and going astray with them in their idol worship, making their idol your idol, and not freeing yourself from their emotional entanglements and the things of the world that are contrary to the will of God forces you to prophesy from a wrong place. When you prophesy from a wrong place, God judges you because your prophecy is a misuse of the priesthood. You are supposed to ministering God to the people out of your priesthood, not your prophecy.

The third type of priest is the one who ministers directly to God. The Spirit of the Lord has insisted that I speak about this again. In the passage we just read, it talks about the sons of Zadok. The sons of Zadok are the priests that replaced the lineage of Eli (1 Samuel 2-4). Remember, Eli prophesied according to his emotions. He did not engage God, even for the survival of his children. He did not pray for them. He just said whatever God wants, that is what will happen. The one good thing that Eli did was train Samuel. Samuel was a prophet and he was a priest as well. Samuel was adopted and being trained in Israel as a priest until the lineage of Zadok emerged. The point is that Samuel was put there as an adopted priest before he was a prophet. Later, when Samuel went to the house of Jesse, he went up to offer sacrifice. You can see that his foundation is the priesthood.

The question is what is a priest? We must understand our role as priests. The priesthood has not passed away. The priesthood is still functional. And if we do not understand how to be priests, we cannot prophesy effectively. The failure of prophecy in this season is because the priesthood has been skewed, misdirected, and misstructured. It has directed toward things and people, not directly to the Holy One. Mainstream prophecy has been coming from the soul and emotion of the people and the influence of things, power, and interactions rather than from the direction of Divinity.

Eli failed in his priesthood because of the same things. Today's prophets have been more interested in having relationships with all the people and the congregation, which is what people in churches want leaders to do. However, the relationship between the priest and the people should not work that way because it always ends up skewing the prophetic message. The Israelites were so attached to the political system of Saul that the house of Eli could not extricate itself even after Saul had fallen. Be careful what you are doing in this season. Otherwise, your prophetic process will be so skewed by and infected by politics that you can never prophesy effectively. You will prophesy only from the emotions of the people at the time. It will never be for God but for the people, their immediate needs, and their fight with one another.

I have written several books that are available. I am recommending Hashamayim 1A and Hashamayim 1B. And the book on prayer called the Golden Cord. This is the time to get them and study them. Also, the book that just came out is on the beatitudes called Opening the Gates of Glory: The Beatific Life.

Remember, you are a son, a priest, and a king. Christ has made you a king and a priest and these roles flow from sonship. Your capacity to prophesy accurately can come only from your priesthood. If your priesthood is skewed, your prophecy will be skewed as well. In the passage we read, it said that those priests who went astray with the people of Israel shall bear their punishment. Their punishment then is to minister to the people. Ministering to the people is not an evil thing. It becomes evil when you accept and are influenced by the structure of idol worship that the people have created. Then you yourself turn things into Divinity and you begin to prophesy to things, for things, and about things. Remember, the second type of priest ministers to the things of the temple, which then becomes a chore. That is how ministering to the things of the temple becomes a punishment. You must be careful because it influences your prophetic capacity. For example, let us say you prophesy about a new car. That is okay because a new car may be needed. It becomes a problem when you are consumed with things and your prophecy works only from that perspective—the need for the thing about which you prophesy. Let me explain further. Maybe you begin to prophesy about political power. Many current-day prophets were wrong in their political prophecy because their hearts and their priesthood were focused on the power—the thing—not on the kingdom. They were focused on immediate power and immediate accolades, saying things that people wanted to hear, and calling themselves prophets.

The thing that you have to understand is that God is not going to completely remove all of them because the scripture says they shall minister in my sanctuary. However, they will not minister to God. They may have thousands or even millions of people listening to them, but the ministry and the prophecy will be directed to the people's inconsistencies, their emotional instability, and their desire and lust for meat. Even the prophecy of a powerful person, as we have seen today, will so draw them towards that power that it blinds their capacity to see whoever or whatever God is removing.

Too many prophets have prophesied falsehood in the political arena, but it was not an intentional falsehood. The falsehood was rooted in a lack of understanding of their own priesthood and, as a result, they prophesied from a flawed perspective. God still allows them to minister. God will take some of them out, but not all of them. He will allow many of them to continue to minister to the people because that is their punishment, at least for a season. They will have to minister to the people they have broken by their own prophecy. They will have to deal with the debris they have left behind in the wake of their so-called prophecy when they did not hear what God was saying. Many people are broken because of the prophets who became priests to people and to things rather than to God and have ended up causing the people to be broken. In fact, they have caused some people to say that they do not believe in prophecy anymore. They will still minister, but as a punishment, because they will be overwhelmed by the people who have been broken by the words they have spoken that did not come directly from God. They are not going to hell, but they are being punished.

The other group is going to minister to things. Ministering to things is dangerous because things have a way of biting back. We need things to function. The kingdom is about people. But is it really about people alone or is it about God? We make that comment a lot. But the kingdom can only be about people if it is ultimately about God.

The third level of priests was the sons of Zadok who replaced the lineage of Eli. The sons of Zadok did not go astray with the people in their idol worship when their worship was all about meat and filling their bellies. The sons of Zadok did not make their bellies into their god. We must be careful not to make our god our bellies. Here is the first thing that happened. The priests who were the sons of Zadok brought the message of God directly from God to the people. Their whole focus was on ministering to God. As our passage says, they shall approach God and minister directly to Him in His holy sanctuary. It may seem that they are ignoring the needs of the people, but it was not so. It may seem that by ministering directly to God, they were ignoring the need for finance or the need for other things, but it was not so. By ministering directly to God and into the being of Divinity, they were creating a radiation by ministering to the light and allowing it to radiate throughout the universe by focusing on the God who is light, on the light that is God, on the light that is the Son, and the light that is within where God dwells.

To prophesy effectively, each one of us must embody the principle of the High Priest within our being. The High Priest focused on God and therefore diffused holiness. He did not do that by bringing back the garment that he used to minister in heaven to the earth. God says the way he went into heaven to minister to God is not the way he must come out. That is what the "show person" says. "Look at me! I have a relationship with God! Look at me! Look at me!" You cannot do that. This is not a time or role where you say, "Look what I can do!" After the High Priest ministered to God, the essence of God flowed into him and into his priesthood and they were moved to cloak themselves in humility. Then they would go out and release Divinity into the people. It always surprised me that God said they shall remove the linens and keep them in the temple before they went out so that they would not minister His holiness to the people. That shocked me. I thought, "Why not? Isn't that what you want people to know?" God does not mean that the people should not be holy. He meant that the High Priest should not minister from the arrogance of holiness, but that they themselves should embody it in their own being as they go out among the people. They will naturally diffuse holiness just by being a priest in the presence of God. Because the law of the high priesthood is so complex and strong, when the High Priest goes into the Holy of Holies and comes out, he ministers directly to God as a way of atoning for the people.

We look to the High Priest to see what a priest actually does. What was the first thing God did with Aaron to prepare him to be the High Priest? He was the one who raised Moses' rod to bring about what happened in Egypt. Still, Aaron first acted in his when the people sinned against God.

> **But on the next day all the congregation of the people of Israel grumbled against Moses and against Aaron, saying, "You have killed the people of the LORD." And when the congregation had assembled against Moses and against Aaron, they turned toward the tent of meeting. And behold, the cloud covered it, and the glory of the LORD appeared. And Moses and Aaron came to the front of the tent of meeting, and the LORD spoke to Moses, saying, "Get away from the midst of this congregation, that I may consume them in a moment." And they fell on their faces. And Moses said to Aaron, "Take your censer, and put fire on it from off the altar and lay incense on it and carry it quickly to the congregation and make atonement for them, for wrath has gone out from the LORD; the plague has begun." So Aaron took it as Moses said and ran into the midst of the assembly. And behold, the plague had already begun among the people. And he put on the incense and made atonement for the people. And he stood between the dead and the living, and the plague was stopped. (Numbers 16:41-48)**

God said through Moses to Aaron, "Go and stand between the living and the dead." Moses did not do it; Aaron had to do it because he was the High Priest. When the people were dying of the plague, Aaron was the one who went into their midst and stood between the living and the dead. Then the plague stopped.

First, a priest is supposed to be a mediator between the people and God. He must be someone who stands between death and life and does not encourage death over the people. At this point, we have not been able to stand between the living and the dead. All we have done as priests is join conspiracies rather than taking our stand between the living and the dead. Does it really matter what is causing death? Does it really matter if it was man-made or not? No. It does not matter to the priest because it is not the priest's job to say who caused it. Aaron was not supposed to go and find out who caused the plague among the Israelites. Aaron stood between the living and the dead because that was his job to make sure that death did not continue. That incapacity to stand between the living and the dead affects the way you prophesy. Instead of standing between life and death and stopping death, you become a prophet of death and destruction and begin to talk about how people will be destroyed. Frankly, prophecy does not go towards life. The only way that a priest functions prophetically towards life is by standing between the living and the dead. You do not have a choice as a son or king or priest. You must be the one who stands between life and death for people. We do not know how to do that anymore. When Aaron stood in that place, he did not make a distinction between one Israelite and another Israelite. He did not say only the wicked shall die. The priest had to stand in the center to stop death from spreading to the people who are still alive.

The second thing that Aaron did was use a prayer censer that he carried around to stop the second plague. The prayer of the priest is meant to deal with the spirit of death and produce life. It is meant to be a healing prayer. When you function in the true priesthood, the Zadokian or Melchizedek priesthood, you can open portals of the movement of God in every dimension. Do you realize that Aaron was not the one who opened the ground to swallow Korah's people? It was God. When Israel gathered against Moses and Aaron, God told Moses and Aaron to step away from this congregation so that He might completely consume them. Then Moses called Aaron into his priestly activity. He told him to take his prayer censer and run into the congregation because Moses knew that the wrath of God was going through the people. So, Aaron took his censer, stood in the midst of the people, and God relented. We talk a lot about what Moses did by telling God to stop so He would not destroy Israel, but we forget how the priesthood worked out the same thing that Moses did. Aaron took his censer, stood between the people, and God's wrath has stayed because the High Priest of God stood there. He did not even say a word. He did not prophesy over the people. He just stood there and the reality and embodiment of priesthood was manifested and the wrath of God was dissipated.

The High Priest also has the capacity to create the opportunity for atonement for the sin of the nation and the individual. The High Priest makes the sacrifice for the sins to be removed, which means that the High Priest's job was to cleanse the people from their folly and foolishness. He was a cleansing being. When he prophesied, his prophecy came from the perspective of life. Do you think it was a mistake that Ezekiel's final prophecy was to bring life to the dry bones? Do you think it was a mistake that Jeremiah's final prophecy was about the restoration of Israel? Do you think it was a mistake that Isaiah's final prophecy was about bringing the whole world together on the hills of Zion? When we do not function in our priesthood, our prophecy is skewed. We prophesy mostly based on our anger and we never create an end to that. In every context, the priest is the one who must re-harmonize the situation. If we function rightly as priests now in this current climate, we can re-harmonize the world that has been broken. We can re-harmonize families that have been divided. We can re-harmonize the heavens and the earth. We can re-harmonize creation itself. When we function rightly as priests, then our prophecy can have the right impact because we can hear God directly and truthfully.

The failure of prophecy in this season is the failure of understanding your priesthood. If your prophecy has proven to be false, then your punishment is to minister to the people that you have broken by those prophecies. That is a big task. And God will help. The shameful thing in this context is that people continue to make false prophecies. They keep saying things after God has already spoken. I knew this was going to happen and I spoke it. The reason I spoke was to warn us so that we could be ready, but we refused to be ready because we refused to be priests. Everyone wants to be a prophet, but no one wants to be a true priest. The priesthood of the sons of Zadok or the sons of Melchizedek is measured by the life of Jesus Christ who stood between heaven and hell so that you and I could find a way to the heart of God. Yet we are standing here prophesying mainly from our hatred. Let me explain something to you. Many people who prophesy about America prophesy from the position of hatred because they are not being priests. You know where your priesthood stands if your priesthood is based on fame, how many people follow you, or how you can convince a million people that California is going to fall into the ocean and disappear. If that is your perspective, then the basis of your priesthood is missing because the priest is someone who harmonizes the universe, as I said before.

A priest can open temporary portals and then close them again. That is what priests do and they are the ones who offer sacrifice. You can offer the sacrifice that was made before the creation of the world and at Calvary as a place of opening up portals of mercy and compassion. Yes, you can open portals of judgment, but your greatest task is standing between the living and the dead and stopping the plague by your presence. Then your prophecy will produce life. Was it not the priest who declared when a person's leprosy was healed? Was it not the priest who met with the sick person to ensure the illness had run its course? The sick person had to go to the priest who would touch him and bring healing. Was it not the priest who made the sacrifice whenever the nation went astray? Even Elijah, in order to be confirmed as the prophet of Israel, had to revert to the priesthood to win over the prophets of Baal (1 Kings 18). He made sacrifices, which is what priests are supposed to do. He did that in order to get Israel to return to God. It is all in the scripture. We are not going to despise prophecy, but we need to know that prophecy can be wrong because sometimes prophecy is based on your emotions, your experience, and what other people experience, especially if you lose sight of focusing your ministry directly to God. Stay focused on ministering directly to God. That way, in the moment of your prophetic utterance, you are ministering directly to God, and not just to human beings. If you are ministering to human beings, chances are your prophecy is going to be based on human emotional instability. If you are ministering to things, chances are that your prophecy is going to be informed by a system or an illusion. Therefore, focus your mind on God and ministering directly to Him, allowing that to be the place where your prophecy goes. Most of you close your eyes, hear something in your head, and think it is a prophecy. However, real prophecy flows from that priestly position where you minister directly to God.

This is the age we are in now. How does a priest open the dimensions of the universe? When God created the world, there needed to be a giving of the life of the Son of God. A lamb was supposed to be given whose lifeblood or "light-blood" was supposed to frame the universe. So, what did God do? The scripture refers to the Lamb of God who was slain before the foundation of the world—before the world was created. That means that in between the manifestation of creation and the thought of God was what we might call a "stopgap" where the Son became a lamb. This is metaphorical. We do not have a language for it because there is no death in Heaven. It is the manifestation of light as the possibility of life. So, the Lamb of God who was the Son of God gave His life before the foundation of the world. The scripture uses the word "slain." This simply means that He became, in a sense, passive so that the active principle within Him could be released, but He had to be slain by a priest. There was a time when I taught that the father served over the son, and I was rebuked by the Spirit. He said, "You have the wrong interpretation of scripture, Adonijah." And I asked why. And He said, "Because a father shall not lift up his own hand and kill his own child. Did you see what I did when Abraham wanted to sacrifice Isaac? I made him stop because a father is not allowed to make the children the sacrifice." Then I was taught by the Spirit that it was Melchizedek, the priest of the future, which is all of humanity, who had done the act of releasing the light and life of the lamb to bring forth creation. Even though God created the world and it was already in existence, the Melchizedek priesthood, which is you and me, humanity, went there as a single individual because that lamb would become our body in the future. So, we were there. We were the ones who acted as priests to slay the lamb that carried the word of God in light to release it into what you now consider creation.

That lamb became the primal foundation before creation from which the thought of God became manifest in matter. In other words, all that we see in creation was released in the moment human beings served as priests over the giving of the life of the Son of God. In our serving there, we released what we needed for the future. When we serve as priests, we open doors for what is going to be needed in the future. However, when we refuse to serve as priests and instead serve as complainers who do not see our power as transformative, we literally shut the door in other dimensions for the things that are supposed to come towards us for our own well-being. If it were not for sin, the release of the life of the Son of God would continue without death throughout all creation. It would be life leading to life constantly.

Let me give you an example of what I am talking about in the reality of creation. How was Eve created? Eve was not created by Adam dying. God put Adam into stasis, opened up his side, and took a spark of life from his body to create the woman as the being who releases life into creation. It is funny that in the creation of the world, man served as the priest for the creation of man. Yet in the release of the creation of Eve, who is the original temporal womb of creation, God served as the priest. He did not serve as a priest unto life, not death. Out of God's priestly activity came this being called the woman who became the embodiment of fertility and the womb of creation, which provides the possibility of the constant renewal of creation by the seed that is put in it. So, when Jesus Christ came into the world, it was humanity that stood over Him at his death and made the sacrifice of His life. We say He died. It is true—He died but when He did, He released life from His life that was His life. Are you getting the point? Humanity, while thinking they were killing Jesus, was in actuality releasing the life that was the life that was His life that becomes our life. The Jews did not kill Christ. It was humanity. Jews and Gentiles were present at the judgment. Jews and Gentiles were present in the garden. Jews and Gentiles were present at the cross. Jews and Gentiles were present at the point of resurrection. Humanity itself served as the priest who released that life in life, life from life, life through life, and life for life. We did that. Now that we are sons of God, we must continuously practice the art of priesthood.

Remember why priests go astray. They minister to the people in their foolishness. They join the people and prophesy to them so that they can get what is good for their bellies. Idol worship comes from priests who, although they may have legitimately come from God, turn away from ministering to God and minister to the people instead. The idol is the result of the foolishness of the priest ministering to the people. That is the real source of idolatry. Oh, that we may learn how to minister directly to God, that we may not be instruments for creating more idols in the world! Remember, the first commandment, "Thou shalt have no other god before Me." If you are carrying an idol, even if the idol is the need of human beings, you cannot minister directly to God because now the need has become the idol that is a hindrance between you and God. The idol covers your mind. It can and does happen to us and so we must constantly shift our consciousness to our direct priesthood towards Divinity. If we do not do this, we will find ourselves prophesying the way we prophesied for the past five years. Now it is coming to bite us in the proverbial gluteus maximus.

The alternative is we will know who we really are. A priest is supposed to stand for the possibility of convertibility. A priest is a transmutational being and functionalist. This means that a priest can shift or turn anyone, if they are ministering directly to God, towards divine consciousness. On the other hand, the priest can shift a person towards idol consciousness. In spite of my critique and what I prophesied, I prayed for Trump every day that he was in office. When God spoke and said he would not win the 2020 election, I was reluctant, but I did not refuse to speak. I remember telling a friend that even if hell was to rise up and touch the sky, he is not going to win. You need to stop the nonsense because you are not functioning correctly in your priesthood. Your priesthood now should be to minister healing and transmutation to broken people or unrighteous circumstances towards righteousness. You cannot do this if your mind is caught up in natural things. This means that you have ceased to be the person God has called you to be. You have allowed temporal circumstance to determine your priesthood.

Here is your chance to be a priest. You say you want to help people; then be a priest. Every human being is convertible and carries the possibility of transmutation towards righteousness. It does not mean that every human being will say yes because they still have their God-given free will. We will learn how to be priests so that when we prophesy, we do so from the right place. We will learn how to be true kings operating in the kingship of God so that when we prophesy, we do it from the right place. We will learn how to be sons so that when we prophesy from that position, we speak from the heart of God. Then we will not speak speculatively about what we just heard in our minds informed by what we think is moral or immoral, or what we do or do not like. We cannot do that. In spite of the failure of prophecy in this season, we are still the ones God is looking for. We are still the ones who must learn how to function here. And until we learn it,

God will continue to teach us and minister. We need to understand our priesthood. There are times when, because of our behaviors or actions, we are subjected to the ministration of things and to people. I do not know how long this current season will last because it will take a long time to heal the people of God and what has happened to them. Nevertheless, I pray that God will hasten the healing so that we can do the work we are supposed to do on the face of the earth and prophesy from the position of true ministration to God. We can stand between the living and the dead. We can put holiness on the people by being humble among the people.

COMMUNION ACTIVATION:

Let us do communion together. We want to take this communion as a way of affirming our powers as priests for the transmutation of creation.

Type the following web address into your browser to participate in communion with Dr. Ogbonnaya and affirm our priesthood:

https://www.aactev8.com/course?courseid=aactev8-media-archives

Then select Chapter 1 Communion. You will need to sign in to your free Aactev8 account.

Communion Transcription

Take the bread.

With all the angels and the archangels, with all the Ophanim and the Erelim, with all the Hashmal and the Seraph, with all the Malachim, with all the Chashashim and the Benei Elohim, with all the strong ones, the Ishim, Father, and the Pananim, with all the Shonanim, with all the Cherubim, with all the creation, with all the trees of the fields and the mountains, and the seas and the oceans, we offer glory to the Most High God. We offer glory to the Most High God. We offer glory to the Most High God. We offer. We offer. This bread becomes for us the body of Yeshua, the body of the Messiah, the rectifying body that we become as members of that body. All of the body of creation will be healed. The body. Oh the body, the body, the body, the body, the body. All that is in creation will be healed. All will be healed. Creation will be healed. Creation will be healed. Creation will be healed. And humanity will be quickened to get to know the God that created through Jesus Christ our Lord. We pray for the healing of the earth. We pray for the healing of the world.

The body of Christ broken for us. (Eat the bread.)

Take the bread.

With all the angels and the archangels, with all the Ophanim and the Erelim, with all the Hashmal and the Seraph, with all the Malachim, with all the Chashashim and the Benei Elohim, with all the strong ones, the Ishim, Father, and the Pananim, with all the Shonanim, with all the Cherubim, with all the creation, with all the trees of the fields and the mountains, and the seas and the oceans, we offer glory to the Most High God. We offer glory to the Most High God. We offer glory to the Most High God. We offer. We offer. This bread becomes for us the body of Yeshua, the body of the Messiah, the rectifying body that we become as members of that body. All of the body of creation will be healed. The body. Oh, the body, the body, the body, the body, the body. All that is in creation will be healed. All will be healed. Creation will be healed. Creation will be healed. Creation will be healed. And humanity will be quickened to get to know the God that created through Jesus Christ our Lord. We pray for the healing of the earth. We pray for the healing of the world.

The body of Christ broken for us. (Eat the bread.)

Take the cup. As He said, "This is my body broken for you and given for you." Then He raised the cup and He gave thanks. Blessed are you O Lord God King of the universe. Now again with all creation, transmute this liquid to become the blood of Jesus, to become the light of His life, to become the infusion of His whole being. We speak. We speak the name Yod Hey Shin Vav Hey, Yod Hey Vav Hey, Eyeh Asher Eyeh. We speak the name El Chai Shaddai. We speak the name El Elyon. We speak the name. We speak the name. We speak the name. We speak the name.

We speak the name Tzva'ot Elohim L'olam Adonai Ha Kadosh.

We speak the name. We speak the name Adonai Melech Elohim Na'ama.

You are our God. You are our Father. You are our King. We raise this cup, the cup of salvation. I will raise the cup of salvation in the midst of the congregation of the righteous. With all the angels and the archangels, we glorify the Lord. May this become for us the life blood of God that we partake of the life of God, the light of His being. We become life, light and we become His love manifested upon the face of the earth. Lord Jesus Christ, you said as often as you drink this, we suffer your death until You come. Father, You have already conquered death. You have already overcome sickness. You have already overcome all these things. We now walk into it. We receive it, Father. You have already brought salvation. You have brought redemption. You have brought reconciliation. You have brought rectification. We walk into it as we take this today. Father, we remember who You are. We remember the voice of your blood, the frequency of that blood, the sound of that blood. Father, the song of peace that the blood brings. We give glory. We give praise. We give honor. Blessed be your name.

The blood of Jesus Christ shed for us. (Drink the cup.)

Amen.

The Lord bless you and the Lord keep you. The Lord causes His face to shine upon you and be gracious unto you. The Lord gives you shalom in the name that is above all names, Yeshua HaMashiach. Blessed be your name, Lord. The blessings of the Lord rest upon you and your family. May you see the opening of the gates and the manifestation of the new things, the new inventions, the new structures coming directly from the Lord as you minister to the God of Heaven and Earth. As you minister directly to Him, may His inner being flow into your being. May you turn around and bless creation and the people around you. In the name of Yeshua HaMashiach. Amen.

True Prophecy

False Prophecy

2

THE FUNCTION OF THE PRIEST IN THE COSMIC ORDER

When priests worship, angels are
silent because the priests are
acting as God's very emissaries.

Peter says that we are a royal priesthood (1 Peter 2:9). When Israel left Egypt, Moses said to them midway through their journey that they were a kingdom of priests to God and that they must not mark or cut themselves because of their priesthood (Exodus 19). Then, of course, we have the great passage in the book of Revelation that deals with the death and the gifting of the life of the Messiah for us believers, accomplished through His blood and personal sacrifice. As I said before, people today have a problem with the blood as if humanity no longer has blood, as if God did not make blood, as if blood does not really have a purpose within the context of light. Now we are not going to kill people, but we need to figure out why the ancients were so strong in their convictions about the power of blood. There must be something about blood. Whether or not we can access what is in our blood without cutting ourselves, whether we can transmute it to the light that it carries, these are the real questions. I believe that when humanity learns to use its blood from the perspective of light to release what is within the blood system that God put there, then the world will change. I believe that the blood is a principle of light that can affect creation.

In Revelation 1:5b-6, the Bible says Christ gave His blood to redeem us and has made us kings and priests to God our Father. This is a very important statement. The priesthood is the foundation of any legitimate prophecy. When prophetic emphasis or impetus is devoid of priesthood phenomena, prophets tend to derail themselves and operate in a way that ultimately becomes illusionary and delusionary. There is a reason why priesthood must ground prophecy.

You may have noticed in scripture that Moses was trained by a priest. Do you remember Jethro? He was a priest! The reason Moses was such an incredible prophetic person who never truly mishandled the prophetic principle and process was because he was trained by a priest who was not caught up in mere phenomena. Jethro taught Moses not to operate with his emotion. When Moses tried to do so, Jethro corrected him. He said in Exodus 18:17, "What you are doing is not good." Moses wanted to turn the priesthood into sitting around and talking to people from morning until evening. And Jethro said, "What you are doing is not good. This is going to kill you." The priest must know how to minister to people yet maintain a certain separation, not in the sense of cutting people off, but rather by maintaining a certain level of objectivity. Let us look at this again. The one time that Moses got emotional and spoke from his emotion (Numbers 20:10-11), it cost him his entrance into the Promised Land. Whenever priests leave their priestly perspective and prophesy from an emotional perspective, they miss what is coming. So, we need to figure out what we are supposed to be doing in this season as those who carry this construct of priesthood.

Since my last teaching on this subject, I have been moving in the Spirit to revisit the same thing I was experiencing when God gave me the idea of the three priesthoods. I decide to go into the heavenly realms to make sure that I am not misinterpreting the things I have seen. I did not see anyone prophesying in Heaven. I wanted to make sure that I have not been missing the point here. Interestingly, I discovered that everybody who is a believer in the heavenly realms was doing priestly duty. Everyone in the heavenly realm was doing priestly duty! That was my biggest shock. All of their utterances came out of that kingly priestly position. Remember, the Bible tells us not to despise prophecy:

Do not despise prophecies, but test everything; hold fast what is good. (1Thessalonians 5:20-21)

I am not doing that. I am emphasizing that we must learn that the primary function of the believer in the heavens and on earth is that of a priest. I say it so strongly, but I am not saying this because of my background. Look at the book of Revelation, for example. It shows us the believers as priestly communities and what their power is in the heavenly realm. The whole book of Revelation is about priestly function. Part of the failure of the many interpretations of Revelation is that the priestly context has been removed from the context. In this way, all of the discussions become speculative "prophetic revelation," whatever that is.

Yet the book of Revelation begins with Jesus Christ appearing in this great place where He is a priest. He is all about priestly phenomena and their structures and processes. We see Christ coming in His full priestly dress. Then He lies down in the temple, in the Holy of Holies, or in the Throne Room as the lamb slain before the foundation of the world—a priestly activity. It talks about His blood over and over and over again. His movement is all about the kingly, priestly movement. Even the people who are saved in the book of Revelation are focused on priestly activities. The believers are said to carry incense, which is a priestly activity.

However, we have looked at Revelation mainly as a prophecy without grounding ourselves in the priestly. And when we do operate as priests, we do it not from the position of ministering to God, but from the position of ministering to people's "need," our own need, or even from the things around us. If we are going to function in the next movement of God, which must be different from what got us into this current mess, we must begin to ask ourselves, "How should we function as royal priests? What does a royal priest look like?"

When I had my revelation and moved into the heavenly realms, I saw believers functioning as priests, carrying incense and censers. One thing I noticed is angels do not keep silent when prophets speak, however, they do keep silent when priests minister. Do you remember this passage?

When the Lamb [Christ our High Priest] opened the seventh seal, there was silence in heaven for about half an hour. Then I saw the seven angels who stand before God, and seven trumpets were given to them. And another angel came and stood at the altar with a golden censer, and he was given much incense to offer with the prayers of all the saints on the golden altar before the throne, and the smoke of the incense, with the prayers of the saints, rose before God from the hand of the angel. (Revelation 8:1-4) [Commentary added]

When priests worship, angels are silent because the priests are acting as God's very emissaries. In other words, they are the essence of God ministering back to God. The priest is a son who carries the essence of Divinity. Now, when Aaron would go into the tent to minister, everyone would sit quietly. It is believed that when Israel acted as priests on earth, the angels in Heaven sat still because the sons were ministering as priests before God. This is a very powerful thing. This ministration to God releases the true prophetic power of the Holy Spirit into creation if it is needed. And remember this—direct prophetic movement on earth is always the response of priestly activity, having touched the altar of Heaven that releases what humanity needs on earth. It is not from one point on earth to another point on earth. It is from Heaven to the Earth.

You can see that the priesthood has a profound connection to the cosmic order of things. If the priesthood is heavenly and eternal, not temporal, then it has something to do with the cosmic order. This means that the priesthood affects how the cosmos is ordered. In fact, a priest who functions rightly actually activates a cosmos where the power of God can be manifested. Let me explain this statement further. In or before the beginning when God created the world, the Bible says that Jesus Christ is the Lamb of God that was slain (Revelation 13:8). For a sacrifice to be offered in this manner, it means that there was also a priest before the foundation. That priest was Melchizedek who is representative of all of humanity because He slayed the lamb before the creation of the world. This humanity had not yet been created, but it was in the mind of God who brought humanity into *il Tempore* before creation. God allowed Melchizedek, as the representative of all humanity, to function as the "releaser" of the life of the original Lamb of God so that, out of the life of the being and the light that He is, the universe was framed and manifested. This means that if you are a priest, you have the capacity to release light and life into creation in order to create worlds. This is the cosmic dimension of your priesthood. If you look at it from that perspective, the creation of worlds is not based on prophecy; it is based on priesthood. In fact, the prophetic in creation comes after the priesthood. The priesthood comes out of sonship and kingship. No one is a priest in the context of Divinity who is not also a son. Likewise, no one is a priest who does not have genetic interconnection with Divinity and who is not also a king. Sonship and kingship are vital to our priesthood.

Sonship, kingship, and priesthood do not go away when you leave this earth or when creation manifests itself. In fact, they are even more enhanced because this combination of sonship and kingship resulting in priesthood makes you a world creator or rather, world releaser—a releaser of worlds. For the Lamb of God to be slain so that through His sacrifice the world could be created, there had to be a priest. That priest was Melchizedek. The order of Melchizedek, as you may have heard me say before, is the order of humanity. That is why Christ had to become part of our human priesthood. This is a very important point. Melchizedek was us (or who we were) before the world was created because it clearly could not have been the Father slaying His Son. The Bible is very clear—fathers are not supposed to have a hand in the slaying of their children (Deuteronomy 24, 2 Kings 14). If you have a problem with this, let me show you. When Jesus died on the cross, God did not kill Him and Jesus did not commit suicide. Humanity took the life of Christ. He gave His life freely, yet humanity raised the knife, so to speak, or the nail or sword or the cross that killed Him. In other words, we served as the overseer at the altar of His death. This is disturbing to many Westerners, but the truth is we participated in Christ's death on the cross because He gave His life freely then just like He gave His life freely before the creation of the world. Nobody took it away from Him. We could not have taken His life if it were not permitted.

The reason death was the result when Jesus was here on earth is because we have not yet learned how to release life without death. The difference between what we did before creation is because, for some reason, we were not yet made manifest and we had not yet committed any sin. At that point, there was no sin. Because everything was pure, we were able to release life to life. We use the word "slain" because of the limitations of our human language. It would be more accurate to say, "This is the Lamb of God whose life was released unto life before the foundation of the world." We as priests, therefore, released the life of the Son by the permission of the Son and of the Father into life. This is what it means when the Bible says,

In him was life, and the life was the light of men. (John 1:4)

Priesthood and the Cosmic Order

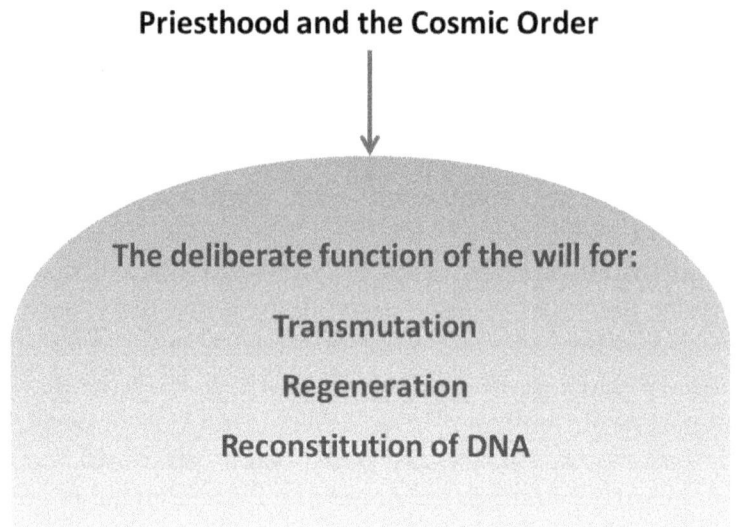

The deliberate function of the will for:

Transmutation

Regeneration

Reconstitution of DNA

We were releasers of light and life in the Son. When He came on this side of creation, rather than releasing life through life, He had to release life through death because death has entered the world. I think we as priests, especially as sons of God, are being called to search out and know and enter into that capacity to release life from life and to overcome this issue of bringing life out of death. We are being called to function the way we did before the world was created to release life from life, light from light, and glory from glory. It was there in the cosmic order before the world was created. This is why I kept reminding us in the previous chapter that if there be prophecies, they shall cease.

I met Ezekiel and I have been trying to develop this animation on what I have seen and how I have interacted with him. He is not prophesying in Heaven. His prophecy is for the earth. It dawned on me that all these great prophets had priestly backgrounds. Did you notice that? Moses was a Levite. He was a priest by his birth. The pharaohs were considered the High Priests of the Egyptian religion and Moses grew up in the house of Pharaoh. Then Moses was trained by a priest later on. We have truly missed something if we have not taken our priesthood seriously. Our priesthood is such an incredible role because every time we act as a priest on earth, Heaven sits silent and listens to us. Angels get quiet. We have talked a lot about the priesthood of all believers, but we have relegated it into trying to predict the future and forecast events. But the reality is that, by operating as a priest, you can actually open up dimensions and direct how things happen, not just forecast it.

A priest is someone who can, by the deliberate function of will, cause things to be transmuted and transformed. By deliberate actions, whether it is called ritual or whatever, the priest changes the atmosphere. Since humanity is the only divine structure on earth that can change its own structure through its own will, walking in true priesthood begins with personal transmutation. So, while on the one hand, we talk about the cosmic order, we also talk about the personal on the other. The priesthood is the capacity that God gave humanity as a divine structure to transmute itself by its will. Everything in the universe has a divine structure, but humanity is the only one that can transmute itself by its own will. This means that your priesthood does not begin with me; it begins with you and the transmutation of your own being and your own mode of action in the world. In other words, your priesthood begins with your capacity for your own personal transmutation.

Every priest in the scripture was supposed to participate in several things in making a sacrifice to rectify what has been separated. A true priest has the capacity to deal with "separation consciousness." In other words, if the priest takes blood and sprinkles it upon the person or thing, atonement shall be made for them. This means that the priest is the one who has the capacity by virtue of their priesthood to bring things that are separated back together, making them "at one." The priesthood creates "at-one-ment." One of the failures in recent world events and in the US in particular is the inability of Christians to create "at-one-ment." They have failed because they did not function as priests. Instead, they functioned as the voices of anxiety and the peoples' problems, fears, imaginations, and conspiracy theories.

As priests, we did not function as atoning centers. Priests must function as atoning centers. We may not always succeed. Nonetheless, if we are conscious of our priesthood, not only can we open up the flow of new creation, we can create "at-one-ment" as well. Every time someone sins against God in the Bible, there is a "separation consciousness." This is true in Christianity, Judaism, and even other religions. It does not mean that there is actually separation, but the separation occurs within the person's thoughts, which then affects their capacity to relate to the whole. When the person goes to the priest, the priest, functioning rightly in their priesthood, removes the separation and brings the person back into the flow of divine consciousness so there is no separation from God. Whenever the priest does not function rightly in their priesthood, they are unable to do that. With all of the division that has happened and is still happening in this country, preachers are still constantly stoking the same division rather than realizing that, as a priest, our job is to create "at-one-ment." This is the first and most basic function of the priesthood in its manifestation on the earth.

Before creation, the priesthood was supposed to release life from life, life from light, and light from light in the person of the Son. The priesthood, which was not even in existence in the way we see it today, was supposed to draw out life and light, and open dimensions for creation to come into being. He was supposed to draw not out of death, but out of life from life, light to light, glory to glory. When we function effectively and come into the true Melchizedek order, we will be able to manifest life in creation without having to go through death. We have not learned it yet, but it is part of the original intent of God for priesthood. For example, one of the first acts of Aaron before he was set up as a High Priest was when he took the censer and stood between the living and the dead. He released life, stopping death in its tracks. The second thing he did after he was installed as the High Priest was thereby facilitating atonement or "at-one-ment." He became the one who stood between the sinner and God. He became the one who performed the alchemy to allow the sinner's conscience to be cleansed so they could find peace with God. The Bible does talk about how some people refused to go to the priest and they carried their sin, but it was never Aaron's place to go around telling people they were going to die. His major job, and the major job of any priest, was to create reconciliation between the sinner and God.

We must learn how to move in a way that allows the people around us to get atonement for sin and "at-one-ment" with God. I say that very clearly because atonement is the vehicle for removing the separation consciousness between God and the sinner so that there is an interflow of being without separation. Only a priest can do that. A prophet cannot do that. There is not one place in scripture where Jesus Christ is referred to as our prophet. Please remember, I say this not because I hate prophecy. I believe in prophecy. I am not a prophet; nor am I a son of a prophet. Yet I am telling you that Jesus Christ is deliberately called out in scripture as our priest and our High Priest. If prophecy was the thing that was vital in our current climate, we would not have failed in the way we did. What is missing is not the intuitive grasping of things. What is missing is the priesthood. We must stop blaming everyone else for how things are and re-focus on scripture.

A priest is a person who carries the crucible for transmutation in a variety of contexts. Let us go back to Aaron. Israel sinned in a variety of ways all throughout the year. Every year, a sword hung over Israel to bring judgment. On the Day of Atonement, the High Priest went into the Holy of Holies and when he came out, all of Israel's sins were forgiven. In fact, the only word the High Priest brought from the Holy of Holies is that their sins were forgiven. That act of going in, finding, and retuning the life of Israel is the function of believers. Now you tell me, how have you been a priest after all the chaos that has been happening in this nation? Rather than functioning as someone who removes the sin of the people, do you continue to exacerbate the problems of the people by constantly creating the same problem, or by constantly prophe*lying* or prophe*cheating* or prophe*fooling*? If that is the case, you have left your priesthood. You are not a place of atonement, a place for the transmutation of people's lives and situations so that sins are removed and people are renewed from the inside. You have emphasized people's anxieties and disappointments rather than bringing healing.

The priest must have the capacity to bring healing to the depth of human hubris. The priest must have the capacity to bring light out of life and make "at-one-ment" to remove separation consciousness from God as well as separation of human beings from human beings. Even though we are sons and daughters of God, our priesthood reminds us of our interconnection with all humanity. We cannot be priests unless we bear the same pain, the same feelings, and the same disappointments and take what is happening to all of humanity into ourselves. Remember, every High Priest is chosen from among their brethren, from people who have the same kind of experience. The Bible even says that Jesus Christ could feel all of our failures and all of our pain. He was not made a High Priest who stands apart from us.

The next step to healing what has happened to the church is to establish priests who become much more concerned about healing the psychic trauma that the people have carried, in addition to the division that has occurred between humans, and between humans and God. A priest's task is to remove that divide and he can only do it through priestly alchemy. Priestly alchemy demands that the priest gets involved in what is happening with people in order to transform it into life, peace, and the glory of God. Screaming and shouting about whatever is happening politically is not going to help you unless you return to what it means to be a priest. Priests were not allowed to deal with only the holy people. They were allowed to make a distinction between the holy and unholy, but they were supposed to take the unholy and make it holy and make the profane sacred. That is the alchemical power of the priest. Any priest whose major task is not to transform other people and the world in this way will fail. When priests fail to transform sinners and to transform the unholy into holy, they begin to prophesy out of their own likes and dislikes. Do not forget that Jesus never said that anyone did not deserve salvation. Every person must make this choice for him or herself. If your prophecy tells you that so-and-so shall not be saved or so-and-so will be destroyed, then you are missing the point and you have ceased acting rightly as a priest.

God designated an entire clan of people to be priests because of its longevity and dealing with humanity according to what it is they need throughout generations. Every priest has the capacity to transmute life. Every priest has the capacity to create regenerative paradigms. We talked about the priest and the removal of the divisive consciousness between human beings and God, and between human beings and other human beings. These divisions hinder our ability to view other people as human beings. A priest deals in this context with the transmutation of the world in which humanity lives by constantly opening portals into the realm of Divinity.

As we discuss the regenerative principle, you need to know that regeneration does not happen by a prophetic word. It happens through priestly activity. If there were no sacrifice and no priestly movement, regeneration would not be possible. You might say that a person does not need a priest to do this. I am not saying you need a priest. I am saying that *you need to be the priest and you need to function as a priest*. Then you will say that a person does not need to do all of that to transmute themselves. Really? How is that working out for you? The reason you and your situations are not being transmuted is that you are not being a priest. Every time you act as a priest within a particular context, it means that you are finally putting yourself in the position of the people around you and you are speaking to them from the possibility of their own transmutation and not from the need for your own rightness. Even the priest must make a sacrifice for himself. If the priest says he does not need a sacrifice for himself, then he cannot actually transmute other things and other people because he is operating from a separation consciousness and acting like he does not have anything within himself that could hinder him from acting effectively. Until we get the priesthood right, we will keep seeing wrongly and prophesying falsely.

I kept wondering why it took Moses so many years to be trained as a priest. Moses is still the most effective prophet we know. Yet he spent 40 years studying with a priest so that his prophetic utterances could be grounded in the reality of the eternal priesthood of the very God whom he was going to serve. You and I say we are regenerated, but our regeneration is not merely caused by us. It is caused by the death and the resurrection of Christ, the ultimate act of priesthood. Even when someone leads you to Christ, they make you go through a process. It is a priestly act. It is not a prophetic act. It is a process whereby you follow a certain pattern and, by priesthood, that person leads you into the activation of your own priesthood.

When God put the priesthood together through Aaron and the other priests, He created a constant opportunity for the reconstruction of the information within the DNA of Israel. Every time the priest acted, there was a sort of "re-information" or inserting new information from another dimension into the life and DNA of the people of God. Priestly activity does that. All those acts are to inform the human DNA with information from another dimension. You will notice in the Bible that although the prophets prophesied and did all kinds of actions, the people were never changed. Have you ever wondered why the people were never changed by the prophets? God kept sending the prophets and the people kept rejecting them. However, once the priests took their positions, the people started obeying. Once the priests stopped acting foolishly, there was no need to raise up a prophet to rebuke them. The priest is the one who understands the structure and movement of

Divinity. The prophet knows how to tell you what is going to happen if you do not keep the commandment. The priest knows how to deal with you when you fail to keep the commandment and bring you back into equilibrium and alignment through the process of being a priest. It is amazing.

I will give you another example. Do you remember the book of Ezra? It always amazes me that people skip over the book of Ezra and go straight to Nehemiah. The real restoration of the people was not the building of Jerusalem. Real restoration came when the priests restructured the peoples' mindsets, redirected them, and brought them back to godly modes of behavior. They restored the right teaching and godly rituals and activities. Ezra, who was the priest, became the founder of the new Israel that came from exile. If there is going to be healing in your house and among your family, you must take the position of being a priest because it can happen only in the context of priesthood. All of your prophetic screaming and shouting will not do anything. You must learn how to be a priest.

In addition, the priest holds the key of Metatron and it is within the role of priesthood that the key of Metatron is tuned. If you and I function correctly in our priesthood, we can open the Metatronic nature within us. Within the construct of that Metatronic principle, we can bring any person, nation, or group of people into it and recalibrate, rectify, reconstruct, and redirect for the purpose of life. The key that made Aaron so powerful was the Metatronic key. In this realm, the priest is the one who holds the key of Metatron. The key of Metatron holds the 12 layers of your DNA with all of the names of God manifested within it. The priest actually holds the key to tuning the layers of your DNA and allowing people to come into attunement with the structure of their own DNA. Isn't that what Jesus did? By becoming our priest, He opened up the key for you to be able to access the hidden structures of Divinity within your own DNA. You are who you are today as a new creature because your priest stood for you. Let me ask you a question. How many times has Jesus prophesied to you? Every day, He functions as your priest, and through this interconnectivity, He constantly tunes you toward what you need to be and what God meant you to be. When you take your priesthood seriously, then your prophetic movement will be grounded in the Divine intent. Then it will not be easily swayed by fleeting contexts and what people are doing to each other.

How do you know when you are functioning in your priesthood effectively? You will know when you begin to draw healing to people. How should we begin to deal with what is happening now? First, a priest must work toward healing people. In doing so, the priest cannot heal only the people he likes. Again, you run into prophetic falsehood because you want to heal the people you like or who agree with your political worldview and what you think the world should be like. But that is not a part of the Melchizedek priesthood. In the Melchizedek priesthood, all of humanity is engaged somehow through it and only those who choose to remove themselves are removed. We do not remove anyone. We cannot be in a place where we do not accept that someone has chosen to remove themselves and then treat them as if they are not a part of that very principle of humanity.

Functioning with the Metatronic key has to do with action. I am avoiding the term prophetic action. Rather, I am going to use an old word that people often do not like—"ritual." Rituals are modes of Divinity for changing behavior, structures, and context. Every time we attach the word "prophecy" to something, we tune it according to our own foolishness. Let us say that there are actions of priests that open up dimensions and possibilities. If we stand as priests with people, we will be able to open up doors for them. How many people are discouraged? Many people are so discouraged right now that it is not funny. Many people are very disappointed and hurt by all this prophecy. We must take a stand as a priest. People do not step into their priesthood because they, unlike prophets, cannot prophesy and go hide. Where are all the prophets right now? They are all silent because they are not functioning in their priesthood. A priest cannot separate himself from the people when things go wrong. A priest is always with the people in both the ethereal and physical realms. The return of the priesthood will be the healing of prophecy.

Next, in order for us to function effectively in this age and the next movement of God, not only do we need to function in our priesthood for ourselves, but also for the nation of our people. It is not just about praying. You must learn how to go in the spirit and participate in priestly activities in the heavenly realm. Every time you take your position as a priest on earth, Heaven is silent and wants to hear what you have to say. I want you to hear this. Your priesthood on earth has a counterpart of priesthood in the heavens. It is made up of the whole community of saints, all of these great men and women, all of these mothers and fathers who are moving in the realm of the spirit. Every time you consciously take a position of priesthood for healing or reconciliation and you stand with your censer and you pour out your incense, Heaven stands with you. When we are conscious of our priesthood, every time we stand in it, all of our brethren in the entire cosmos stand with us because our priesthood is a cosmic priesthood.

The twelve keys or the keys of Metatron are available to anyone who will act truly according to their priesthood. While there is a person who became Metatron, Metatron is also a principle by which Heaven actually creates transmutations and opening of dimensions. Every priest, by virtue of their priesthood, including you, is a portal and someone who opens or closes portals and gates. The priest functions as one who can open dimensional, spiritual, ethereal, or psychic portals, and they can also close wrong portals or gates. Whenever you see that certain things are happening in society that should not be happening, someone somewhere has opened up a portal or a dimension. As a priest who is fundamentally interconnected with divine cosmic ideas and movements, you can stand in your priesthood, and then when you speak prophetically, you can shut down those doors and gates so that they do not have an effect.

We have failed woefully as a body because we have been too emotionally caught up in what we wanted and not in what humanity needed. Remember, every priest has this capacity. If something is not happening, it is not because God has not made you a priest. It is not happening because, rather than strengthening your priesthood— especially in the order of Melchizedek—you have instead chosen to talk and talk a lot. All that talking has not really done anything for us. Do not be discouraged. Instead, find a way to reconnect with your own idea of priesthood especially as it seats you in the order of Melchizedek for which Christ is now the High Priest. Find a way to reconnect to that. Ask yourself, "How do I use my priesthood to bring healing to the context in which I now find myself? How do I use it to bring reconciliation among brethren?" Unfortunately, some people are literally reveling in the division in the Body of Christ. Their stubbornness does not allow them to be Christ for others. Rather, they say, "I am right no matter what anyone else thinks. My position is right no matter what." If people suffer and die, it really does not matter to them as long as their position is constantly proven. You see, this stance is part of what contributes to false prophecy. However, even a prophet must be willing to say, "Hmm. I really do not want things to happen this way for the sake of the lives of the people." Remember, every priest is chosen from the people so that he can relate to their suffering and their personal experiences. Then the priest can take that very thing to the throne room of God and bring it to God as a ministering instrument. When any religion fails in its priesthood, it means that it is time for it to die and a new breed of priests must arise. You can never remove priesthood completely from any system of religion or faith. If you do, the religion ceases to exist. That is why you have so many Pentecostal churches start and then die because it has been based on a prophetic word rather than the priestly structure.

In Judaism, the people with the keys of the names of God were the priests. There is a reason these keys were given to the priests. The keys to the names of God were keys to the DNA and the psychic structure of God's people. They were trusted with being able to use these keys not to manipulate the people but to redirect them toward the original Divine intent. As a priest, you carry that Metatronic key. The first is the key to the *mystery of being* which is hidden in your being. The key to being is the great I AM. I AM of life. It is the key that deals with all of the structures of your being. What did the High Priest do on the Day of Atonement from the moment he went into the Holy of Holies until he came out and pronounced the unmentionable name? As he spoke the name, all of Israel's sins disappeared. One of the laws in scripture is that you can never use the name of Yod Hey Vav Hey as a curse, yet you have believers who use the name as a way of speaking and putting curses on people. You cannot combine that behavior with being a priest. The priest was always for the people. I want you to go back to scripture and see that the priests never did that. The prophets were free to do that because they were not carriers of the people. The people always disobeyed the prophets. God knew what He was doing. So, when God wanted to redeem, He sent His Son as a priest.

How have you been dealing with your brethren who disagree with you? Have you dealt with them as a priest or have you continued in this prophetic nonsense even though it did not come to pass? Step back a bit and ask yourself if you are functioning properly within the priesthood of Melchizedek, of which Christ is the head. Are you really functioning the way Christ functions? People who think they know better will look at this and say, "What about this or what about that?" All I am telling you is that your prophecies have turned out to be false, so repent, and go back to your position as a priest instead of trying to make excuses. It will not work.

As my close friends will recall, I said when Trump won the election in 2016 that it is a judgment to prove what is in the heart of the church. It is not about Trump; it is about the church. This is the judgment of the church. I wish I was wrong, but that is where we are, especially in the evangelical and Pentecostal churches. It is such a terrible thing that has happened to the followers of Jesus. But the people have decided that the Democrats are god and every decision they make is godly, all the way from abortion to lifestyle nonsense. I am not even talking about Democrats. I am talking about those who actually claim to walk in righteousness and demand that we reveal our priesthood. Their priesthood has become a service at the altar of Satan. It is true. You can tell because they follow things blindly and anyone who disagrees with them is a problem. Many of these people have gone their own way and they put what people want to do over what the scripture says. So, we have that issue, but sometimes you correct the people who are open to correction and who want to take the position to change the world. I am telling you that the real priesthood is no longer in existence in the body of Christ. We need to retake our positions as priests. In doing so, we will be able to change and transmute the world and cause a renewal of creation.

The next thing I want you to notice is what Aaron wore on his body as the High Priest. His clothing was an imitation of the Melchizedek body. It was also the transportation device for the priest to go from one dimension to another, interconnecting dimensions, and opening up portals. In fact, whenever the priest is in his priestly garments and stands on his priestly triangle or square, there is an immediate interconnection from that point of their consciousness and the whole of the cosmos.

When I went into that realm, I spoke with the Lord and said that I wanted to know what the priesthood is like. I often ask questions like why are our prophecies failing us so much? That is how I learned some of these things. I saw whom I believed to be the Lord in the vision, and I saw Aaron. It was amazing. Then I saw all these priests and all the believers were dressed with ephods and brilliant garments. All they were doing was waving incense. The smoke from the incense was pure white. As they were waving the incense, I watched their intent manifest in creation. This is what the priesthood of believers can do. Not only can they rectify creation, but they can manifest the Divine intent and the intent of the believer if it is connected to the Divine in creation. What really surprised me was each of them could create a world in the amazing movement of that smoke. It is hard to explain. Call it a vision or whatever you want, but that vision of a priest being able to open up portals for the manifestation of new worlds, new patterns, and new structures and interconnections between worlds told me that we still have a long way to go in our priesthood.

The next thing is that when a priest functions in the fullness of who they are, they can get to the point where they can become an oracle. When the scriptures talk about the priesthood and the temple and altars, it also talks about oracles, never about prophets. The true priest operates in the oracular principle. We are in a new place. Prophecy will look different from now on. It will not go away for now, but prophecy will cease one day. And prophecy can fail. Our priesthood, however, is established forever. Brothers and sisters, I want to encourage you that just because prophecy has failed does not mean God has failed. Just because people saw wrongly does not mean God has failed. Step back and function in your simple priesthood and see what happens. Think atonement. Think of yourself as a transmutational instrument for the redemption of humanity, for the salvation of humanity, and for life. Please hear me. This is not for the salvation of your political party because it is not going to last forever. In reality, it is also passing. Political systems will fail, but your priesthood is what stands still. Whatever happens in your nation, if you know that you are a priest from God, you can create patterns for the transmutation of your own land, your own family, and your people. That is what Jesus did.

Since then we have a great High Priest who has passed through the heavens, Jesus, the Son of God, let us hold fast our confession. For we do not have a High Priest who is unable to sympathize with our weaknesses, but one who in every respect has been tempted as we are, yet without sin. (Hebrews 4:14-15)

Every priest has the capacity to make propitiation and for standing for the people towards God, not towards a human being or anyone else. Whom are you facing as a priest? Turn around and face God as a priest. Unless we do that, we will watch our people suffer because we have not done what we are supposed to do. May God help us!

When priests function rightly, the eyes of their thrones open. It is in the context of priesthood that those eyes are opened because priestly activities and behaviors allow them to open. The whole body is filled with those eyes and the eyes of the body of the priest can look and see in every direction. It is in functioning correctly as a priest that the universe opens to us and we see what is happening in those realms. An incredible change has entered creation and I am praying to God that we do not miss it. We must be careful because we could be used to create something that is not new but is dangerous for humanity. Much of what we have seen in creation is the result of people who are beginning to be priests who end up using their priesthood to support an ideology rather than the cause of Jesus Christ. When Christ becomes secondary and the word of God is put on the side, systems are created that make us more important than Christ. We have to be careful.

COMMUNION ACTIVATION:

We want to take this communion together as a way of affirming our powers as priests for the transmutation of creation.

Type the following web address into your browser to participate in communion with Dr. Ogbonnaya and affirm our priesthood:

https://www.aactev8.com/course?courseid=aactev8-media-archives

Then select **Chapter 2 Communion**. You will need to sign in to your free Aactev8 account.

Communion Transcription

Brothers and sisters, take your communion wherever you are. This is a priestly act.

The Lord Jesus Christ took a piece of bread and He said, "This is my body." A repetition of the original act. When Jesus gave that bread, He hadn't shed His blood yet. But He said, "This is..." before He actually died on the cross which means the essence of this is beyond the physical reality of blood. It is in the spiritual realm, the very essence of who God is. "This is my body, given for you. Take it."

We take this to the glory of the Father, and the Son, and the Holy Spirit.

[Eat the bread.]

He took the cup and He gave thanks. And He said, "This cup is the new covenant in my blood. Take you. Drink you all of it and do this in remembrance of me." Receive.

[Drink the cup.]

By faith, we receive the essence of the life of the Son of God. Life into life. Light into the light. Grace into grace. Lord, we take our position as priests of your kingdom, as a kingdom of priests. We receive with thanksgiving. We receive for the healing of our nations. We receive for the healing of our families. We receive for the healing of our tribe's tongues, and all the nations of the earth. We receive for the healing of the sun, the moon, and the stars. We receive for the healing of the ocean, of the earth, of all the planetary systems You have made. Lord, we believe that Your healing flows through all and we stand here as the priests through the blood of your Son. We receive and we stand for the nations where we are located. For those of us who are in exile, we receive for the nations from where we've been exiled. We raise all to the glory of Your name. Blessed be Your name, Father. Bless Your people, each one that has listened. Teach us, God to be true priests so that when we prophesy, we prophesy from the position of truth, the position of service to You, from the position of true priesthood. Blessed be Your name, Lord. Hallelujah, Father. Bless Your people again, we pray, in the name of Yeshua HaMashiach. Amen.

Brethren, praise God!

3

PRIESTHOOD AND THE ALTAR OF FIRE

> When the priest does not walk
> in Love, Wisdom, and Divine Will,
> the fire becomes destruction.

Let us look at some scriptural principles of what it means to be a priest. This is what God our Father has made us—kings and priests. Our priesthood is real. We just need to understand how it functions. The way to keep ourselves authentic and grounded is by constantly remembering and understanding how our priesthood works. The Bible is very clear that the priesthood has been given to us for all eternity. If Jesus Christ our Savior, Yeshua our Messiah, is a priest forever in the order of Melchizedek, then we all are priests in this order. I will talk about the priesthood that God gave Israel that was implemented in the Torah and the Tanakh. Then we will shift to what that means for us and how our priesthood is supposed to function, especially at this time when there is so much uncertainty for some people.

Let us talk about the priesthood and elemental principles. I am not talking about elemental spirits but rather, elemental *principles*. One of the first things you notice from reading the scripture is that priests work with the altar of fire. This is in Leviticus and Numbers. The scripture even talks about not offering "strange" fire at the altar of the Lord. Some translations refer to it as "unauthorized" or "profane."

> **Now Nadab and Abihu, the sons of Aaron, took their respective firepans [censers], and after putting fire in them, placed incense on the fire and offered strange fire before the LORD, which He had not commanded them. And fire came out from the presence of the LORD and consumed them, and they died before the LORD. (Leviticus 10:1-2 NASB) [Commentary added]**

We know that Abraham was a priest before he was a prophet because he built altars for the Lord. We may talk a lot about how Abraham was a prophet, but we forget that one of the first acts of Abraham, when he came to the land of Canaan, was not to prophecy but to build an altar. Why build an altar? It is not just a piece of stone but an opening of gateways, portals, and pathways. Without getting too complicated, every priest must serve at an altar and has the capacity to build an altar. An altar is a position where you make your offering or where you open up a portal between this realm and other realms. One altar can open one gateway, depending on who builds it, or it can open up several pathways and gateways so that things from other realms can come into this realm. We know Abraham was a prophet and I know my people constantly talk about the prophetic. However, God did not just establish the prophetic in Israel even though Moses was a prophet and we have used the Word as a prophet. I would like to argue that Moses was first and most importantly a priest and that his prophetic movement grew out of his priesthood. He was trained as a priest and this is why he was able to implement the priesthood in Israel. Moses was also a king as it says in Deuteronomy 33:5 that he was "king in Jeshurun."

A priest serves at the altar of fire. The reason he does so if you are reading the testament of Jesus (New Testament), you notice that Paul says that our God is a consuming fire, not that our God has a consuming fire. There are at least three ways to look at the consuming fire from what I have said.

One is that God is so pure that the fire around Him cannot stand anything that is evil and is impure. So, God consumes all impurities. Everything that comes toward God and comes into Him is purified in the fire.

Another one is that God is a destroyer. You know that God can judge. However, I do not think that the whole context of God being a consuming fire in the Book of Hebrews is that God kills people. True, if you approach the fire in the wrong way, it will kill you. But holiness is intrinsic to the consuming fire—it makes things and people holy. So, the altar of fire is for the purification of the world.

In ancient times, when some people were baptized into mystical Christianity, the first thing that was said to someone who was baptized and entered into the mystery was, "Let the earth and the water and the air and the fire be your servants to draw you closer to the heart of God." This was said to the person who was being initiated into Christianity— someone who was coming into priesthood. New Christians were told to "let these elements be your guides and lead you closer to God's love." The priest serves at the altar as a way of releasing the fire of God's love into creation. I know your conception of the altar is about death, but really it is a metaphor for the release of another life where a life gives its own life upon the altar through the principle of fire to allow some other life to be renewed.

So, the priest operates in the elemental. Now you might say to me that everything in the universe has some form of fire, which is the principle of life. Every living thing has a fire burning in it, which means that the priest is a sustainer of the life of living things within creation. If you go to Leviticus (or Numbers), it says that the priest always puts things through the fire. The idea is that the priesthood controls the fire that flows into life. That is not enough. The priest does not just serve on the altar of fire because fire alone, as an elemental principle, can become destructive. If the priest is connected to the divine elemental flow of creation, then the priest must be a giver of life. Now we know that on this side of man's experience, you cannot have life without death, but there is a realm where life gives forth life. It is not in this realm now. But by operating as a priest at the altar, we can find a way to open up dimensions and we can actually minister from life to life, not from life to death. The elemental principles of the universe are under the control and power of those who, in reality, will serve as priests. It is in your Bible:

"I baptize you with water for repentance, but he who is coming after me is mightier than I, whose sandals I am not worthy to carry. He will baptize you with the Holy Spirit and fire." (Matthew 3:11)

The time is coming when you will be baptized with fire. The way you can interpret this is when the fire came into the temple, it consumed the offering, but it did not kill the people. There are places in scripture where it talks about fire killing the people, but I want to talk about this in the context in which the priests were ministering. When the fire comes within the context of priesthood, it consumes what is being offered, but it does not destroy the offeror. So, the ability of the priest to control this elemental thing means that it can consume what you are offering *per se* but also the sin that you are offering from your life. It consumes, but it does not consume you. This was the first revelation that God gave Moses.

**Moses saw the bush ablaze with fire, but it was not consumed.
(Exodus 3:2)**

It is so different from how many of the prophets operate. Moses saw the burning bush. It was burning but not consumed. Do not forget that Moses experienced all of these things as a mentee of a priest.

As a priest, you shepherd this elemental principle of fire. This is more than fire. I am talking about certain forces of the Divine that operate in the world that, if not directed and controlled by the presence of the priest, can consume the world. God raises you up as a priest so you can control it. It amazes me. God has made you a priest. A priest ministers at the altar. A priest directs the flow of the divine fire, which means that the priest directs how the flow of the power and nature of God goes into nature. When the nature of God becomes destructive, it is because the priest has not been at his position. What exactly did God want from Aaron, his family and the Levitical priesthood? Why put them at the altar of fire? They sustained the world and directed the energetic flow of Divinity within creation at this time because there is evil in the world. Without the priest standing at his position, evil will consume the world. If evil tries to consume the world, the power of God or the nature of God will take off its self-imposed limitations and destroy the world because God cannot stand evil. Let me illustrate this further. You believe in Yeshua and that because of Him the judgment of God does not come upon you. Why? Because He is your priest. The High Priest of Israel was extremely important. Even everything he wore meant something. All of the letters in the Hebrew alphabet were in the Shin Gadol, which was also in the face of the High Priest. The same structure that God used to create the world embedded itself in the intellectual point of the High Priest as a way of allowing the High Priest to connect with how God created the universe. In this way, every time the High Priest entered into the altar and offered fire, he recalibrated the world toward the original structure of Divinity.

So, the elemental principle is fire. Every Christian should understand baptism by fire. I am bypassing the discussion of water right now to discuss elemental fire deliberately because the concept of fire as the principle that gives light and life to the universe is under the auspices of the priest. Again, fire alone does not give life because of its tendency to consume. The Bible talks about how Aaron's two sons offered strange fire at the altar and fire came from the Lord and destroyed them (Leviticus 10:1-2). If you offer fire to God, it must carry the nature of God and His nature consumes it into Himself. However, if it goes against the nature of God, the fire that you offer will turn back on you because it cannot stand the purity of the intrinsic nature of Divinity. Again, it is the job of the priest to distinguish what is purified fire and what is defiled fire.

The Bible says that God makes His angels spirits (or winds) and His ministers' flames of fire (Hebrews 1:7). The priest is a minister of God. He is a flame of fire. The priest operates on the altar of fire. That is not the only thing the priest does, but it is important to understand these concepts. The fire allows the priest to build walls of protection around people. The problem we have as believers is that we say all these things, but we seem to be incapable of operating as priests to protect the people who need protection. We are so busy complaining about children and women and the broken-hearted not being protected, but we are not operating as we should. If we were literally building altars of fire, then we would be manifesting messengers. As God says,

Of the angels, he says, "He makes his angels winds, and his ministers a flame of fire." (Hebrews 1:7)

We are the ones who, as priests, open the gateways for beings of fire to enter creation, not for destruction but for purification. There is going to be judgment, but judgment must become subject to the principle of repentance and fire that comes from God carrying mercy. The altar of Israel where the priests worshipped was an altar of mercy, grace, divine purification, and the embrace of the Divine. What kind of priest are you? Are you the type of priest who goes around looking for what people have done wrong so that you can destroy them or are you the priest whose fire is purifying?

As a priest, you serve at the altar of God, which is the altar of fire as well as the altar of transmutation. You bring the impure to the altar that becomes the crucible for transmutation. Humanity has turned the fire of God into the fire of destruction. When man discovered that fire was destructive, he began using it, not based on the divine nature but based on their desire. So, the fire that the priest controls can be poisoned by their desire or it can be empowered for transmutation. Their desire can move upward or downward or it can become imbalanced when it is not centered on God. This imbalanced desire is what makes people misuse fire. In fact, this is how people can go from using fire as a light to using fire as a destructive force against humanity. The reason we have destruction by fire in creation is due to the actions of the priests, all the way from the ancient Zoroastrians, the Hindus, the Africans, and the Mayans. The only people we know that did not use fire in their religion are the ancient Egyptians. This misuse of the fire is a distortion to enslave other people. The priests channeled God as a vendetta against people they did not like. Be careful.

As a priest, you will operate from a position where you manifest the unconditional nature of Divinity. Some may use this altar as a way to bring fiery beings to destroy everyone who disagrees with them. The fire will judge by its own self if it is used rightly. When I look at the life of Abraham, I think, "Who am I to argue that his first activity in Canaan was a priestly activity?" I look at Moses and I realized that he was the one who stopped God from completely destroying Egypt. Every time Pharaoh cried, Moses asked God to relent. Yet I keep watching so-called evangelical or Pentecostal priests who do not intercede for the world, but only for those who agree with them. That is not being a priest. You must intercede for the people who do not agree with you because it is about the multi-cosmic and multi-versal principle of all the worlds. Remember that I said that the difference between a Jew and a Gentile, if you want to use those terms, is that the Jew believes in one God and many worlds, and the Gentile believes in many gods and one world.

So why does God baptize the believer with fire? It is because you are the director of the elemental principle on the earth. You decide how it is going to work and how you will use the fire. If we are to operate as priests who control the elementals, we must be aware of three things:

1. The Divine Love
2. The Divine Wisdom
3. The Divine Will

We must be grounded in all three things that we find in Christ in the New Testament and the life of Moses. We must operate in these three things to divine the elemental principles.

Let us say I am operating within the context of Melchizedek and my father Aaron. I must also operate within the context of Divine Love. This love is so demanding because love is what infuses those elementals to keep them from destroying those who have erred. Remember that the priest is the one who stands to create "at-one-ment" and peace between God and the people He has chosen. The principle of love is at work here. Love is not about whether you like or dislike someone. You may not agree with them, but you do not have divine permission not to love them. Every priest must learn this principle. In Western religions, you cannot forget that the Catholic priest listens to the confessions of both his friends and his foes. This is something that Pentecostal and Evangelical priests cannot do. We know that Catholicism has killed others for its principles, but I want to discuss the ideal that is being offered here. The Catholic priest will forgive. He will minister to others, regardless of their agreement with him.

What does it mean to be a priest and operate in this triangular principle of Divine Love, Wisdom, and Will? Some have gone so far as to say that the three wise men who came to worship Yeshua at His birth embodied these three things. Indeed, it is by embodying Divine Love, Wisdom, and Will in their right construct that you create a crucible for the transmutation of people's lives. The priest must always work within Divine Love, Wisdom and Will. When a priest does not walk in that, the fire is not directed towards transmutation; it is directed towards destruction. Remember, transmutation is changing something from one nature to another. When love becomes hatred, people say someone is lost. But actually, it is when this hatred becomes a desire to hurt. It is all about desire. When wisdom becomes foolishness, the priest operates from a materialistic perspective without looking into the people's hearts and only at their mistakes and folly. In that case, you have created a structure that is grounded in the earth rather than in heaven.

The Triangular Principle of Divine Love, Wisdom & Will

Heavenly Foundation

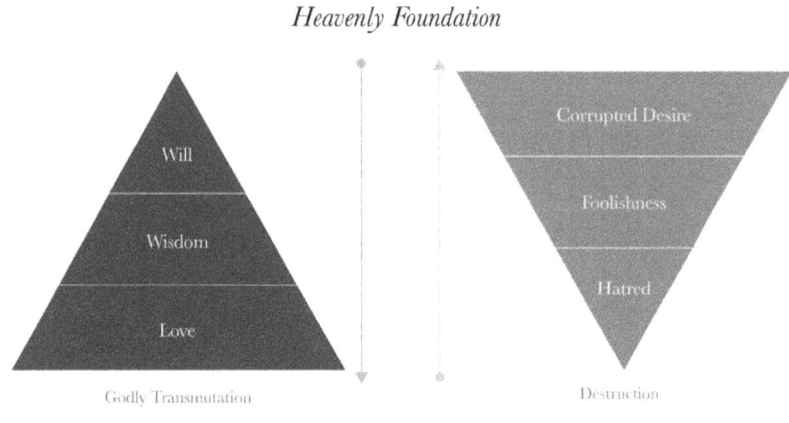

Earthly Foundation

This is a complete distortion of the priesthood because it becomes power organized by hatred. It becomes information organized by control and then the will becomes a mere desire towards greed. When that happens, you now have this trinity of transmogrification through which things or people are corrupted. All of these things are manifest and shown by the ancients and the simple playing cards that they have left for us. They are showing you how these things operate in the world.

Because many of us look at everything from an evil perspective, we miss the point and do not ask the right questions. Why did our forefathers leave all these games for us? Why did the African fathers leave the game of going from one house to another on a board on the ground? Why did they leave the ancient game of hopscotch? These are ways to train the priest to be grounded in the original mysteries that God left His children upon the face of the earth. Yet to us, we regard these things as evil because we do not want to learn about the work of the priest. The priest is the one who does the great work. If I open an altar, I am baptized with fire. If I open an altar of prayer, then I create a gateway for beings of fire to show up and for higher, finer realities of life to be manifested where I have created the altar. You will notice that when you begin to pray and intercede for people and you influence the atmosphere with that intent, then suddenly the atmosphere will be infused with energetic systems. The priest then becomes the one who releases messengers of fire to create the crucible for transmutation. No matter what is happening now in the US, we must move to the position through which we operate as priests. The prophetic is not going to cut it in our current condition. We must come back to creating the crucibles of priestly fire.

And while staying with them he ordered them not to depart from Jerusalem, but to wait for the promise of the Father, which, he said, "you heard from me; for John baptized with water, but you will be baptized with the Holy Spirit not many days from now." (Acts 1: 4-5)

In His own ministry, Jesus Christ controls and directs the elemental principle of fire. In the Torah, a person brought the sacrifice, then the priests prepared it, then they brought it before the High Priest and burned it with fire. Why? They burnt it so that the aroma and the fragrance would rise up to God. The rotten part of the body and the interior structures are cleansed and burned. What goes up in the fire is the essence of the being in exchange for the life of the person who offered the sacrifice. There is a need to actually understand what a priest does at that altar and in so doing, the very essence of Divinity flows back to the people and turns them into messengers of fire, purifying fire, and fire that carries divine fragrance. We really must understand that we are being called to be such priests.

Usually, the goal when serving at the altar of fire is that fire drives itself into creation so that the atmosphere where the priest is serving becomes a reflection, even minimally, of the heavenly realm. If you notice in scripture, the High Priest, the secondary and tertiary priests, and everyone in Israel must offer sacrifices for themselves. In other words, they must offer fire for their own purification. The reason that we want to talk about this elemental principle is that the fire of mercy, repentance, and grace that God Himself releases allows us to operate in a way that brings Heaven down. We can talk about how, in fact, when the sacrifices were made at the altar of fire in Israel, beings were seen all over the land while they were making sacrifices and opening the fire realm in the temple. Everyone all over Israel saw that.

We are using fire as a metaphor and a symbol of a finer reality in the realm of the spirit, in the pneumatic and ethereal realms. The heavenly flame burns and comes down. It enlightens the darkness, burns the dross, and causes the gold in our being to become reflective in this world. Did you ever ask yourself why Israel is free for a whole year after every festival of fire (Day of Atonement) when the High Priest goes into the temple and comes out? It becomes a reflexive principle of Divinity and the people are free to serve God and go about their business for a whole year. If the High Priest did not do that, then sin would pile upon sin. For those of us who know Yeshua and believe that He is the Messiah, we must come to the understanding that He ends His ministry as a priest in the order of Melchizedek serving at the altar of fire in Heaven where we are co-priests with Him.

If the earth and creation are not moving the way they should, it is because the priests are sleeping at their posts or they have tried to force things into being through prophecy without standing rightly in their role as priests. I have shown you that a number of the Major Prophets in scripture came out of priesthood. I was reading the other day and realized that Daniel was not called a prophet. He was called a seer. I began to wonder about that. Daniel was one of the few prophets who was not from the priestly line, even though he became a king. But everyone else is called a prophet and you can see the priestly line in their backgrounds. I would suggest to you that while we were busy talking and not being at our posts as priests, people were enslaving children and creating all kinds of havoc because there was no one creating an altar to facilitate the purification of the nation and of the world. We are complaining about these things happening in the world, but where were we? As priests of the land, we allowed those who serve other gods to become the priests of the land. They did what they do in their own priesthood. We must take our position in the order of the Divine One and follow the priestly principle that allows the fire to come down for the transmutation of our world.

When the priest does not walk in Love, Wisdom, and Divine Will, the fire becomes destruction. The movement of the elemental principles of the earth becomes an earthquake. The movement of the wind becomes a storm and the movement of the water becomes a flood.

Thus, the reason we need priests is to balance the elemental structures with each other. Then the universe in which we exist can be transmuted back towards the divine gold. This is who we are. This is our job as sons, kings, and priests. This is not about moving little elemental spirits and moving them around in your backyard and thinking you are doing something. This is not about making little creatures whisper and talk to you. Those kinds of things do nothing for the world. This is about being in the realm where the Divine pours out His being and His original nature into your vicinity because you have opened up a world. By opening up that world, you direct the Divine thought and power into the world for its sustenance, transmutation, rectification, and continuous manifestation of God's original intent when He was creating the world.

The first thing to understand is that you can open up an altar of fire that creates messengers of fire because you were baptized with fire. The first act of Christ was to baptize you with fire. He never baptized anyone with fire. You were baptized with fire and the fire is only destructive when you bring the wrong fire towards the altar and you refuse for it to be purified.

When we operate in the fire, then the Metatronic principle can begin to manifest in creation because it is embedded in our being. The fire that we operate in contains the fiery alphabet, if you will, by which God released light into the darkness. So, the priest becomes a releaser of light and an opener for messengers of fire to come upon the face of the earth for transmuting the earth from darkness to light, from destructive desires to desires of love. Remember why your priesthood is important because the Messiah you believe in, in the person of Yeshua, becomes the High Priest according to the order of Melchizedek. The mystery of fire is within the context of your priesthood. The mystery of fire was with Aaron and it is with Jesus Christ, our High Priest.

COMMUNION ACTIVATION:

We take Communion. It gives life upon the altar to release life to those who need it. We take communion because someone gave His life for us and paid the price for us to be here. This is something women should understand because they make so much sacrifice with their own blood and their own bodies to bring us into this world. And the priest is the one who serves at the altar where the transmutation takes place, where life gives birth to life. We are getting to the point where our priesthood is not going to be the giving of life out of death but rather life out of life in the future. Therefore, we begin with the One who says, "I am the resurrection and the life," not I am the death and the resurrection. I came that they might have life and have it more abundantly, not I came so that they could have life out of death. The priesthood that we are getting into is the priesthood that controls the elemental principle as it relates to the fundamental nature of God so that the world is rectified back to the fiery principle, which is the actual intrinsic nature of God. It is the principle of light and the purifying, life-giving element carried by the vessel of love. We want priests who heal the world, who create light in the world and bring forgiveness into the world. We want to bring reconciliation and transmutation until the world comes into a brighter day. Our call and our service on this altar are to open up dimensions so that the fullness of Yod Hey Vav Hey will come down upon the altar. When it does so, it turns the whole of creation into an altar—ergo, drawing down the fullness of Divinity. Then the kingdom of this world will become the kingdom of our God and His Messiah. And on that day, the Lord will be one and His Name will be one and humanity will be one. Blessed be the name of the Lord.

Type the following web address into your browser to participate in communion with Dr. Ogbonnaya and affirm our priesthood:

https://www.aactev8.com/course?courseid=aactev8-media-archives

Then select **Chapter 3 Communion**. You will need to sign in to your free Aactev8 account.

Communion Transcription

Take the elements.

Today we will focus on the blood of the Lamb, which is the light and the fire. We are serving at the altar of the life that God gave for us, the life that becomes of the enlivening process in our bodies. We know that the night that Yeshua was betrayed, He took the bread and said, "This is my body. Eat this in remembrance of me."

[Eat the bread.]

Take the cup.

Blood is the light and the fire. Every sacrifice that was made was comingled with fire and blood. The fire was the principle whereby the original essence of fire within the very life of the being that was put on the altar was drawn into the fire and dissipated throughout the universe to rectify the universe and for the person for a while. In this case, what we are doing is we are using this altar of the original sacrificial person of Melchizedek, which is all of us before the creation of the world. We are raising this cup with Yeshua. This cup is a renewing covenant in His blood. And since I teach that the blood is congealed light, then on the altar this blood becomes the essence of the being of God infusing Himself throughout creation. If God is a consuming fire and the fire that consumes the offering upon the altar turns it back into the nature of the One from Whom it came, it fills everything. The time is coming when there will be no need for death in order to produce life. We have come to the point where life must produce life. Grace must produce grace. Mercy must produce mercy. Forgiveness must produce forgiveness. May God help us as believers as we do this. This is the blood of Christ that was shed for you and is the elemental principle of the fire. The wine represents the redness of the blood, and the blood represents the fire of God congealed within creation and now released by the priest who serves at the altar. Amen. Hallelujah. Praise you, Father.

[Drink the cup.}

4

ADAM'S PRIESTHOOD, OUR PRIESTHOOD, AND GOD OUR INHERITANCE

When the lamb was slain before
the foundation, it was not the
destruction of life but rather the
release of life into creation.

This book is meant to quicken you into your priesthood so that true prophecy may flow from your being. In order to do that, we must talk about the priesthood of Adam of Genesis 2—not the failed Adam from Genesis 3 and 4. God created the universe as a habitation for part of His being. We know that God withdrew Himself, yet remained, to make a space for creation to exist. He used His word to surround creation because His word is expansive and His word is Himself. God made the space within Himself to create the world and therefore placed creation within Himself. Within that space, He also created all manner of things including the heavens and the earth. They are not God and not larger than God. God is not circumscribed by them. He is a great, all-powerful, merciful, glorious being within whom, as Paul said to the Greeks in Acts 17:28, "we live and move and have our being." This incredible and marvelous God permeates everything and without Him nothing is or will be sustained. Everything that is sustained within creation can only draw from that being. Even those we do not like draw their sustenance and their being within creation through Him. By that fact, they are within Divinity and move within Divinity and by His power.

God made a statement before making Adam.

Then God said, "Let us make man in our image, after our likeness. And let them have dominion over the fish of the sea and over the birds of the heavens and over the livestock and over all the earth and over every creeping thing that creeps on the earth." (Genesis 1:26)

The priesthood of Adam gives us a clue as to how we are supposed to do certain things. Even the creation of Adam is a manifestation of the various categories of priesthood. In fact, in the first creation narrative in Genesis 1, God combines the priesthood and kingship. Then in Genesis 2, God creates humanity and you know how the story goes. God gathered all the principles and all the essences that God had made in creation that were in relationship with Divinity and He used the dust and the particles of all that to create Adam. Adam is the summative principle of the whole universe. Everything is in Adam. Thus, Adam became the crucible for the transmutation of creation. Likewise, a priest is also the crucible for the transmutation of creation. In the second creation narrative when God made Adam, the Bible says that he was made out of the dust (Genesis 2:7). Adam became the reason for the atmospheric structuring of the earth. Adam became the potentiality for the atmospheric transmutation of any planet in any galaxy or any place that God made. This is because Adam was created to be the one who carries the moisture of praise, life, worship, and Divinity to activate the potential Divinity in all of creation. So, any place humanity goes in creation, we carry the water of God with us. By our presence, atmospheres are transformed.

We always look at the idea that man is fallen, but we tend to forget that humanity actually carries the imprint of God's hand. God placed human beings upon the earth to allow for the peopling and activation of other planetary systems. All the systems that can contain life will need human life in order to move them to the level of Divine intent. To that end, God made Adam from the galactic or cosmic particle through the gathering of all things. In other words, God took a pattern from all things that exist and created Adam. Again, Adam became the crucible for the transmutation of creation, but also for its beautification. If Adam goes wrong, all of creation goes wrong. Adam affects all of creation, especially in the lower realm.

Let us look at some things that a priest is supposed to be doing. When God created Adam, the Bible says that God placed the man He had made in the garden east of Eden (Genesis 2:8). I submit to you that this garden was the first temple and Adam served as the priest of that temple. Adam was placed in the garden, which was a microcosm of the universe. It was the temple's center. It was the *sanctum sanctorum* or the Holy of Holies of all creation and Adam was placed there to serve as the High Priest. However, he was a High Priest without having to sacrifice blood because there was no death in the garden. He used the offering of supernatural light as a way of creating life in creation. Adam served as the messenger of light, as the one who embodied Divinity within creation. It is out of that placement in the microcosmic temple that Adam was able to prophesy the nature and the future of all living things. He was able to prophesy into existence the hidden nature of all creation because the Bible says this:

Then the LORD God said, "It is not good that the man should be alone; I will make him a helper fit for him." Now out of the ground the LORD God had formed every beast of the field and every bird of the heavens and brought them to the man to see what he would call them. And whatever the man called every living creature, that was its name. The man gave names to all livestock and to the birds of the heavens and to every beast of the field. (Genesis 2:18-20)

Do you realize that, as a priest, Adam had only perception? He saw things in their potentialities. Then, by his word, he named them. This naming prophecy is so powerful because the Bible said that whatever Adam called them, that is what they were. Remember, Adam was operating in a pure and harmonic state with all creation at this point. So, when he spoke the name in that original "garden language," it was in the language of Divinity unadulterated by corruption. When he spoke that prophetic word, it caused all the animals to be.

All of the things that we see in creation today—birds, beasts, and those that are extinct—were framed and formed in this world by Adam. They were created by God, but their manifestation in creation was spoken by Adam. God permitted Adam to speak that way, which means that Adam had to give part of his word or his essence for things to exist in his world. When Adam sinned, everything fell apart because his essence was in all of birds, beasts, etc. Consequently, Adam's descent became the descent of all creation because his word was in them. God permitted Adam to frame them according to his word. The prophetic principle that Adam carried in framing the world according to the pattern of his being and intention is so clear in that passage. The priesthood of Adam served him to be able to pattern creation according to his intent. Remember, God did not tell him what to name the animals but brought them in their creative state to Adam to be formed or manifested in this realm. Those of you who know me understand that I draw a distinction between creation and formation. Adam participated in the formation, but they [the animals] had already been created even though their pattern here on earth had not yet been set. So, Adam was placed in the *sanctum sanctorum*, the Holy of Holies, which is the garden. As a priest and from the vibration of his words and his being, he was supposed to affect all of creation. He was supposed to make all of the worlds have exogamic planets so that they could carry life. Life was supposed to flow from him. Part of the responsibility of the priesthood that God placed on Adam was to sit in the Holy of Holies and look into what God was doing in the heavens. Remember, God passed all the animals before Adam. He was to sit in the Holy of Holies, see the patterns of Heaven, and manifest them on Earth. Adam's priesthood is our example in the same way that we know Jesus Christ is our High Priest who was initiated into the order of Melchizedek.

God built the temple, which is the garden, and God placed Adam there. Adam is the ultimate inner sanctum of Divinity, which means the priest is actually the Holy of Holies because it is in him that God breathed and God created a *neshamah*, an intellectual principle within Adam that could communicate and connect with Divinity. So, you have an inner Holy of Holies that Adam carried and you have the garden that was the temple. It was not really like the temple and the ark that was the Holy of Holies in scripture. It makes sense that the Lord Himself made Adam the Holy of Holies because, if He lived inside of Adam, putting His breath and His essence in Adam, He had to have made Adam the Holy of Holies.

The High Priest of the temple was the Holy of Holies because the Holy of Holies remained useless until the High Priest entered. It did not communicate because the intertwining principle was that the ark represented the ultimate Holy of Holies that a human being is supposed to be. Adam, within the context of creation, was the *sanctum sanctorum* because the breath of God lived in him. Thus, when he spoke from that center, things took shape in creation. I will go even farther and say that the power to frame how creation manifests flows from the inside of the priesthood. However, what is inside the priest must be divine, must be Divinity. If the priest carries wickedness or destructiveness rather than the Divine, then his ministration to the world results in wickedness and destructiveness as well. Right now, some preachers are calling for civil war in the nation, but in doing so, they are functioning as mediating priests of Satan and the destruction of humanity rather than of God. Does this mean that I do not believe in judgment? I do. But part of the basic structure of a priest is to harmonize creation. We are called to bring forth a new creation. In the garden, Adam did not have to kill and he manifested what was inside of him. The harmonic structure of creation—the fact that the elephant is held together, for instance—was because Adam spoke from the place of divine coherence. Remember the scripture.

And he is before all things, and in him all things hold together. (Colossians 1:17)

Adam spoke from that perspective. Hence, whatever he spoke into creation represented and reflected who God is, how God made him, and who he was within the context of the temple of the garden. Now the temple of the garden repeated itself throughout all creation, but the garden was the microcosm of the cosmic temple. God does not ask us to deal with the whole universe at once. He did not do that even with Adam. God had given Adam dominion within a specific place in order to train him how to have dominion over all of creation.

A priest does not serve humanity only. A priest serves God. We tend to forget that a priest is for creation itself to keep it in consonance with Divinity. Adam gathered all of the reverberative frequencies of all of creation and offered them to God as worship while simultaneously holding creation in balance. If you notice, our priesthood in this current age does not really focus on harmonizing creation and nature. On the contrary, we have turned our priesthood into judgment and destruction, telling people to buy guns so that they can kill other people. This is not the true essence of priesthood. Oh, I know you are going to say Israel did a number of things that went against God, but you are talking, in that case, about an imperfect priesthood. You are talking about a priesthood that is infused by human self-destruction.

Do not forget that. Your priesthood is not from the lower realm. Moses did not kill anyone by his own hand. He offered animals and sacrifices, but not a human being. Adam, in his ministry, operated mainly in the structure of life. Likewise, Aaron did not kill anyone. A priest must keep his hands clean from the blood of others. Now when there is war between nations, a priest can serve God, open doors, and have access to the army of God, but he himself must keep his hand clean. We know that one day, Jesus Christ, our High Priest will come to judge the earth and that we are under Him. However, the structure of His priesthood was life unto life. Jesus told his disciples to buy swords, but when Peter tried to use it, what did Jesus do? He told him to put his sword away:

Then Jesus said to him, "Put your sword back into its place. For all who take the sword will perish by the sword." (Matthew 26:52)

It is important to balance scripture.

I know many of us do not want to talk about how the earth is groaning or that rivers are dying. In traditional African culture, we would say that a river is dead and caution people not to drink from that stream. Even in the Bible, it says that they could not drink the water in some places because the water was poisonous. A prophet who acted as a priest could put something in the water and the water was healed. This is what Moses did. He made the bitter waters (marah) sweet (Exodus 15:22-25). As a believer, you can take a cue from the priesthood of Adam as someone who is the basis of the transmutation of nature to keep it functioning at a level that gives human beings life. I am sorry, but praying for trees to live is not superstition. Speaking life to the streams in your country is not superstition. Speaking to the atmosphere to ensure that we are breathing clean air is not superstition. It is not liberalism, leftism, or rightist. It is the right thing to do because we are the priests.

If we live with inner turmoil, we cannot do our priestly work very effectively. People who do not focus on God because they are afraid of losing something are ineffective in their priesthood. We know that people have killed each other throughout the generations to get material things, but a true priest of God harmonizes the universe.

In Israel, the priest was in charge of dividing the inheritance for the people. Why did God not trust Joshua alone to divide the inheritance?

First, Moses divided the inheritance before he went to the land. He saw the land in the Spirit and divided it among the children of Israel. Joshua and the High Priest divided the inheritance and gave each family their inheritance. The High Priest was present for this process. In the same way, you and I, if we function rightly in this creation, should give every family of the earth space to function according to the gift God has given to them. We should be the ones opening up the divine inheritance to all the families of the earth so they can draw from and contribute to creation in the way they were meant to. We should not ever be the ones to wipe out a people completely so they are not able to manifest their inheritance, like the Aryan priests did in India. I know what you are thinking, "Well, God told Israel to wipe out all the Canaanites." Did Israel actually wipe them out? No. If you remember, those same people that Israel did not wipe out became part of the lineage of the Messiah that you worship. I want you to think about that because Bathsheba was a Hittite. So, Israel's priesthood, by being a vehicle to cleanse the world of idolatry, was still the opening for the redemption of the world. If God is so interested in you being a priest who kills the people around you so that you alone may obtain your inheritance and retain the power that you think you have, then why would God say that the time is coming when we will beat our swords into plowshares (Joel 3:10)? Everything we do is temporal. Yet if we operate rightly as priests, many of the conflicts upon the face of the earth will be gone. I place our current conflicts, this destruction, and chaos at the feet of the priests of the world. It is when priests do not function correctly as God intended that they begin to function based on their own selfish gain to raise and keep power. When priests have these corrupt motivations, chaos thrives in creation. Oh, that we would find priests who walk in harmony within themselves and operate in the original intention of God! In spite of all the things we do, we are not manifesting the original intention of God. We are manifesting our national selfishness or our tribal animus. We must move beyond that and begin to function as priests who harmonize creation.

Do you think it is okay for you to cut down a tree that contains a hundred tons of water and not plant another one just because you are a Christian? Those of you who want to say that there are no problems on the earth, go and watch the growth of the desert in Africa. Some of you will say the problems there are because Africans are cursed. However, you must remember that the problems we have in Africa are due to the failure of priesthood. We have named so many things in creation from a demonic perspective that it is no wonder that our waters are becoming poisonous. Our trees are dying from their roots because our priesthood has not functioned correctly. We restore the priesthood of Adam. We love talking about the garden east of Eden and the waters that flowed in it, but there was a person there who was a priest. God gave to Adam the power to uphold the garden with the harmonic frequencies of his voice and with the vibration of his being so that it affected all of creation. The priesthood of Adam has given us all the things around us that we enjoy like the trees, the birds, and all of nature. We must renew our priesthood and it must speak to creation. For example, unless our priesthood speaks to the sun, its radiation will one day harm us. That is not how it should be. No, "the sun will not smite us by day nor the moon by night" (Psalm 121:6). We must create that shield by our priestly harmonization. God has given priests things to do. However, when priesthood becomes "priest-craft," it becomes a problem because it becomes a means to manipulate people to gain power. Anyone who calls you now to pick up guns and weapons to kill other people is trying to use your blood to establish their family as leaders upon the face of the earth. Be careful how you allow people to prophesy to you in that way. Now self-defense is different, but that is not where we are.

The priesthood of Adam meant that he sat in that temple of the garden as the Holy of Holies and, from the center of his being, he framed how the garden should repeat itself within the earth, outside of the earth, and into all of creation. In that context, priesthood meant dominion and changing ecosystems—"eco-dominion," if you will. It does not mean eco-destruction. Eco-dominion refers to directing the flow of the energetic principle of Divinity so that the dominions of the geographic realm and the nested states of ecology receive life from the priests. They receive the life of God that is in the priests. The priest activates the original presence of the essence of the Divine within creation so that creation begins to worship and bless. Then the priest can gather that praise and send it as an offering into the presence of the Holy One. Thus, is the priesthood of Adam. Remember, I said that Adam is the one who harmonized creation. God literally passed all the animals before him. Now I am going to say something that is not in the scriptures. I believe that God also passed by Adam all of the other seeds of creation, before they became the fullness of what they are because God wanted the essence of Adam to be in all of the things that are made. God wanted Adam not just to see these seeds of creation but to have a harmonized interaction with them from the breath of Divinity. In doing so, all creation was connected. If that did not happen, we could not talk about "all creation is waiting for the manifestation of the sons of God" (Romans 8:23) because it draws from how creation was framed from the being of Adam. Therefore, when Adam shows up in his rightful place as a priest, creation will come. So, sonship is connected to priesthood and prophecy flows from sonship and priesthood. Any prophecy that does not flow from sonship and priesthood is divination.

The High Priest divided the inheritance with Joshua, the king, for all of Israel to make sure that each one had their inheritance and their space so that they could manifest what was in their DNA or what the Holy One had implanted in each family. We can understand from this that every family of the earth has a gift God has given them to bring into the world. Every family and every clan of the earth has an angelic structure sitting over them or with them. When the destiny of the people is not followed and the people begin to go against the divine intent for them, the angel of their being is weakened. This is what happened to Israel. Even Michael could not defend Israel when he refused to walk according to his destiny. All of this is dependent on how the priest functions. The priest must leave the gate open and create an atmosphere for harmonization, atonement, reconciliation and interconnectivity. The funny thing is, if we do not raise creation to its highest levels by our vibration and by our prayers and worship, then creation will become destructive to us too because it loses its inhibition and its interconnection with us.

Let us come back to this issue of inheritance. If you notice in the Hebrew scripture, you see that the Levites and the priests had no inheritance among their brethren. For reference, read Numbers 18: 20-25; Numbers 26:22, Numbers 35-36, and Deuteronomy 10:9, 12:12. 14:27-29, 18:1ff, and 32:8-9. Let me summarize what I am trying to tell you. We have discussed creation and how you are the distributor of the inheritance or the one who opens up the inheritance to the families of the earth. Rather than being the destroyer and a hindrance to the families of the earth, you become one who helps them frame their potential so that God is glorified through the tribes, through the family, and through the households of the earth. He is the God who must be worshipped by all of the families, but the priest whom God has raised must be the one who keeps that door open and helps them stay open to that potential. The priest must not be partial. We know that priests are drawn from a particular tribe of people, but Adam was not the kind of priest who was partial to cows or elephants or trees. He was the type of priest who gave all creation an opportunity to manifest the divine intent outwardly. He formed them according to the pattern from which they were created. He manifested them according to the utility for which God created them, so they continue to harmonize creation and gather up the essence of worship to the Holy One. How could Isaiah tell the trees of the field to clap their hands (Isaiah 55:12)? How could David tell all the earth to worship the Lord unless he knew that when he spoke as a king/priest, creation answered? How could he understand that the priest was the worshipful leader of the cosmic choir, leading the sound of the harmony of the spheres of the universe? Of course, we know from reading the New Testament that Yeshua is the reconciler of all creation. Indeed, He is the reconciler, harmonizer, and the one who causes all the cacophony of voices you hear to become a symphonic orchestra of worship. The priest brings those elements together. In the act of priesthood, we direct the sound of creation towards the throne of God. We guide the flow of worship into the Holy One and, in so doing, release the rain of abundance and increase upon creation.

The Bible then says that the priests of Israel did not have an inheritance among their brethren:

> **And the LORD said to Aaron, "You shall have no inheritance**
> **in their land, neither shall you have any portion among them.**
> **I am your portion and your inheritance among the people of**
> **Israel." (Numbers 18:20)**

David says that they were given the tithe. I want you to notice that the priests were in charge of the tenth. The tithe or the tenth is a symbolic process of creation and perfection, which is ten or 1 (One) 0 (Zero). They were in charge of the circle and the one. In other words, they were in charge of moving something out of nothingness. The priest is a carrier of creation. That is exactly what Adam did. God created and brought to formation and then manifestation. This was all by the power of God, not from Adam's power. God passed all things in front of Adam for the purpose of manifestation. The tithe was not just given to the priests so they could eat. It was also given for the purpose of the tenth. God introduced the principle of the tenth in Genesis to make the priest the keeper and an overseer of creation's harmonic movement. This means that the priest, when functioning properly within his role, can stand from that priesthood, stop the destructive storms, and redirect the flow of nature for the productivity of humanity.

The priest was supposed to burn all of the parts of the beast that belonged to God, allowing it to flow up in the smoke as a fragrance to the Lord (for instance, Numbers 15:3). When God smelled the aroma, He remembered. The aroma brought the remembrance of the plight of God's people into His presence. This does not mean God forgets; He does not forget. But a memorial is a memorial. Humanity offers the memorial to bring creation's memory back into harmonization and in this way, creation, families, and human beings are renewed.

Did you know that the priests were in charge of creating the atmosphere for Jubilee? They blew the trumpets, made the pronouncements, and declared the year of release. No slave was forced to remain a slave (unless they chose to remain so) after the priest made the declaration. Because we have emphasized prophecy so much, we forget that the prophetic outflow of the priesthood is what affirms freedom. Jesus came not just as a prophet, but to offer on the altar of the priesthood His prophetic ministration that grew out of sonship and priesthood.

Again, the Bible says they had no inheritance among their brethren. Then it says, "...for the Lord is their inheritance." I want you to think about this for a second. First, why would God not allow the priest to have an inheritance among their brethren? It was because God did not want them to be so attached to their brethren's material possessions and their position that they could not make a clear-minded decision when it came to the worship of God. It does not mean that God wanted the priests to be poor and not have anything because God turns around and says, "I am their inheritance." If the Lord is the inheritance of the priest, then the priest does not have to be afraid of the people who will not give their money when they speak the truth. This is what happened. God knew that if the Israelites went into idolatry, the first thing they would do was threaten the priest and say that they would not take care of him. So, God said, "You will not have an inheritance. I will take care of you. I will provide for your every need." He also told Israel to provide for the Levites through the sacrifices and through the tithe. All of these are important for creating a harmonic interaction between the priest and the people.

As believers, we are all priests, but we are not all called to do the same things. God still calls some people to do certain things. Some people travel around the world preaching the Gospel and have to depend on believers, but they are still mostly dependent upon the Lord. If you are a priest and you follow what people think because your prosperity or abundance is attached to them, you will fail in your priesthood. If you follow leaders and attach your priesthood to leaders, you will fail in your priesthood. If you fail in your priesthood, you will fail in your prophecy. If you are to have relationships with leaders in the world, you must remain independent of them, even though you are connected to them. Your priesthood must not function based on their approval or disapproval. Your priesthood must function only from your direct relationship with God. What happens if a nation decides to go astray? Must a priest follow that nation and go astray with them? The answer is no. The only way the priest can maintain his integrity with Divinity is to remain unattached from the pattern of provision that the world gives.

Does that mean that the priest is supposed to be poor? No. Many believers say, "Well, I am a priest, so I am not supposed to have anything." However, look at what God did to meet their needs. He provided six cities for the Levites called the Six Cities of Refuge. In their failure or destitution, men can always find refuge in the cities of the priests. In this way, the priest becomes a place where failed human beings can come to have their lives rejuvenated and be safe until the time of their release. As a priest, you function in the world to raise a refuge for the weak, the suffering, and the stranger. But what we see today is the priest who does not want to make a space for the stranger or the weak. In fact, we see many priests who say all kinds of things about the widows and the orphans and who treat their workers badly. You would be surprised how many so-called preachers or Christians mistreat their workers. They claim to be such incredible people yet completely mess up the people who work with them. This is serious. Do you think that the people who work for you do not deserve for you to care for them when they have problems? The way that we have structured this world is not the way the priest is supposed to structure his household. There are certain things a priest is not supposed to participate in, yet this has all been kept quiet. For example, the High Priest in Israel was not allowed to own slaves. People were supposed to participate and serve them voluntarily.

Your inheritance as a priest then is God, the Holy One. If you claim to be a priest, where is your inheritance? Your inheritance is God, which means you will never go without. You will always receive supply and your supply will always be full because God never operates from lack. He is El Chai Shaddai, the Almighty Living God. He stands with you. God says that Israel is God's inheritance, then God turns around and says to the priest, "I am your inheritance." That means if you function in your true priesthood, you have an access to the provisional fullness of Divinity. You do not have to be afraid that you will not be supplied for because the fear that your supply is going to fail is a temptation for you not to be a real priest.

So, God provided six cities for refuge and then He supplied another 42 cities where they could live. Then He gave them miles of free space around each city to keep them separate from all other cities. That city was used as a center for spiritual work to keep Israel moving. He gave them 42 cities in which they could live plus six cities of refuge, which equals 48 or 12. Twelve is fully representative of Israel, but it is more than that. God set up these cities so that Israel's priests could control the star systems. As the nations were divining in the stars, the priests could frustrate what the nations were doing to try to redirect the stars or bend the sun and the moon towards the hurting of the earth. Israel's priests were actually protecting the whole realm. Many thought they were just protecting Israel, but they were literally protecting the whole world by redirecting the force of creation away from idolatry, destruction, chaos, and sickness.

The easiest thing to do as a priest is to condemn people because you can see their weakness. It is easy to release judgment because you know their guilt. However, God has called you to heal the brokenhearted, bind the wounded, be the balm of Gilead that brings healing to the nations, and do your best to stand in the presence of God on behalf of the people. You are out of line if you tell people not to pray against things that are coming. You are out of line if you tell people to buy guns and draw them away from praying. In that case, your priesthood has become sorcery. Be careful about what you are doing. Our priestly focus must be for the healing of the nations and the world. If the world continues to rebel against God, then they have to face the judgment that is coming. But in the meantime, our job is to work towards harmonization and atonement. When they left Egypt, Israel did not kill one Egyptian—God did. God knows how to judge righteously and rightly. Human beings do not know how to do that. The priest then must be the one who provides balance for the earth and stands for creation, mercy, and grace. When God decides to judge, we do all in our power to shift that judgment away. There are times when we cannot shift His judgment, but we must not gloat or rejoice in God's judgment.

Our priesthood can hold up creation. Your priesthood is so firm in creation that your inheritance is the Holy One Himself! If your inheritance is the Holy One Himself, then you do not have to be afraid of losing out. You can function freely in your priesthood and, in doing so correctly, abundance will flow to you. You become this balancing principle by mercy, by grace, by focusing on divine "at-one-ment" and divine reconciliation with humanity, by vibrating the frequency of harmonizing cosmic voices towards praise and adoration, and by becoming the crucible for the transmutation of creation even for those who are contrary to you or supposedly your enemies. If you harmonize the earth, then your enemies will benefit from it. However, if that is your fear, then you cannot be an effective priest. Remember, the woman said to Jesus,

She said, "Yes, Lord, yet even the dogs eat the crumbs that fall from their masters' table." (Matthew 15:27)

You cannot be worse than the world that allows everyone to eat, including the animals. I am not calling anyone an animal. This is a metaphor. As a priest, when you harmonize the universe, everyone, even the wicked, participates. If your fear is that the wicked will benefit, then you will not be able to do anything. Your priesthood must be like the nature of your Father who allows the rain to fall upon the just and the unjust until God Himself decides it is time for judgment. Even when it is time, the priest cannot stop crying out and speaking for the people. Again, creation will listen to you because you are a priest.

Provision will come to you because you are a priest and because the Holy One Himself is your inheritance, which means all of creation is bent towards provision for you. You do not have to fear that you will not have enough. That is not even in the books. You do not have to fear that because you function as a priest, your business is going to die. In fact, your business will thrive because your priesthood is directed to God. Your inheritance, even in your business and the work you do, is God Himself. God will not abandon you because He is the one who made you a priest through the blood of His Son. Do not be afraid of functioning in your priesthood for your family, brothers, and sisters. Creation will listen. Provision will flow. You can open doors for the families of the earth to begin to experience the fullness of Divinity's original declaration, which was, "It is good and God saw that it was good." There is goodness in all of the families of the earth, which is the intent of Divinity. Our job is to pray for that goodness to be manifested in creation. Divinity is inserted into all of the galaxies that carry a potential for the manifestation and diversity of life. Our job is to vibrate in such a way that this hidden Divinity answers to the Divinity in us as the priest that serves in the temple of the Holy One.

This is a key. Let us keep the harmonic frequency that Jesus gave us:

Peace I leave with you; my peace I give to you. Not as the world gives do I give to you. Let not your hearts be troubled, neither let them be afraid. (John 14:27)

Walk in that peace and that harmonic interaction or co-inherence of the goodness and harmony of God. Then we can vibrate it into creation through Jesus Christ. As Christ said, "My peace I give to you, not as the world gives." Let us walk in that within ourselves so that we can be effective priests for creation especially here and now. Be the believers who function from that innermost harmony. Are you struggling with a situation in your home? Then be the crucible that causes that situation to transmute as a manifestation of Divinity within your context. If you fight on your own, it will not come to pass, but if you are a harmonic open space, a crucible for the movement of Divinity, it will cause the atmosphere of your family to harmonize. It will begin to attract the beauty and the grace of God, and a deep healing for your people, your brothers, your nation, for those interconnected with you, and ultimately for all of creation. I encourage you to think from your priestly perspective. Then your prophetic capacity will become even more powerful. If you are a gifted prophet, your priesthood will make your prophecy more precise and more powerful. If you are a seer, you will see more clearly by refusing to be partial and operating in your sonship and priesthood. Then your role as a seer will allow you to know what to do. The power that you carry as God's priests on earth is so incredible!

You are so blessed! You are so kept, O priest of the Most High! Your inheritance is the Holy One. Do not be afraid. As long as you keep that in mind and vibrate towards it, provision will flow because God said it. God did not create you to be a priest so that you could be lonely and sit alone as a single blade of grass. He created you to be fertile and to draw water from the Holy Place, O priest of God, O son of God. Child of God, be encouraged. We are going to begin to see a new kind of prophetic movement among believers—not these prophetic words that come out of the bane of fear and some sort of intrinsic hatred of other people. We are going to see a harmonic, formative, manifested, divine grace upon the face of the earth.

COMMUNION ACTIVATION:

Let us take this communion as a way of affirming our powers as priests for the transmutation of creation.

Type the following web address into your browser to participate in communion with Dr. Ogbonnaya and affirm our priesthood:

https://www.aactev8.com/course?courseid=aactev8-media-archives

Then select **Chapter 4 Communion**. You will need to sign in to your free Aactev8 account.

Communion Transcription

You are a priest in the order of Melchizedek. You are learning about your priesthood. The night before Jesus suffered, He spoke the language of priests. This is my body given for you. Do this in remembrance of me. The priest was the carrier of the memorialization of Divinity and caused people to remember the covenant. As you do this, remember me. Every time you take communion, you affirm your priesthood because Jesus said to take it, but now you are the one doing it. In some churches, they say you are manifesting a sacrifice that opens a dimension of the life of the Son of God. He said, "This is my body, broken for you. Take it in remembrance of me." Jesus is saying, "Memorialize me. Remember. Let it be activated in your memory that I made a way for you." You hold that bread in your hand, O priest of God. You hold that bread in your hand, O child of God. You feel the power of the Holy Spirit flowing through you and running up and down your body. You feel the goosebumps that are caused by the movement of the Spirit upon your body. In your body, there is presently a reconstitution of the body of Christ. We are the body of Christ. We are the body of Christ. We are the body of Christ, joint to joint, and we draw life from life. Glory be to God! Thank you Lord.

He took the cup and He gave thanks. He raised the cup and He gave thanks. Blessed are you, Lord God, King of the universe, who gives drink sustenance and quenches the thirst of all those who come to You. Blessed are You! We thank you. We thank you. We thank you. With all the angels and the archangels, with the Ophanim and the Erelim, with all the crowned ones, with all the ones who take care of the depths and the heights, with all the sounds of the heavens and the sounds of the depths, we bless the name of the Lord. With all the flashing thunders and lightening, with all the fiery ones, the Seraphs who sing your praise, with all the Hashamayim, the appearing and disappearing ones, Father King of Glory, with all the princes of God, Michael, with all of them, Father, we worship, we magnify, we come through this blood, through this cup of the covenant. We give praise to you, Father, with all the sons of God, all the children of God from all the ages, we come together, and we worship with those above and those below. We worship, we magnify, we glorify you, O Holy One. Yod Hey Vav Hey Elohim, we worship. By the blood of Yeshua, by that cup of the new covenant, we come into Your presence. With all the victorious ones, the army of the host of Yahweh, we worship, we magnify with all the sounds of praise and magnification. Blessed is your Name! Hallelujah! With all of the angels of the Face, with all of them, King of Glory, with all those who gaze upon the glorious majesty of the Holy One, with all of the force of the foundation of the mystery of the Holy One, to the Son, we worship. With all the Cherub, we worship, we worship. We raise the cup of praise. We raise the cup of salvation. We bless your Name, O Yah. We bless your Name, O Yah. We bless your Name, O Holy One. Praise, praise, praise to the Father. Praise to the Son. Lord, we come through the blood of Jesus. O blood of Jesus, speak for us! Speak for our world for peace. Speak for mercy. Speak for grace. Lord God Almighty. Speak for creation. Speak for the rivers, the springs, the mountains, the hills and the valleys. Speak, King of Glory, for all You have made. Speak, King of Glory that the sun will be healed and the moon will shine. Speak, King of Glory, that the stars that your light, your life, the word You spoke and said, "It was good" might reverberate in creation again. We thank you. Lord, we are so grateful for your life of the covenant. Cup of life. Cup of grace. Cup of mercy. Receive.

Hallelujah. Praise you, Father. I bless you. I praise God for you.

5

PRIESTHOOD AND
THE CHERUBIC PRINCIPLE

The cherubic structure makes it possible for ordinary things to become an attraction for what God made in heaven to come to earth.

Let us talk about Isaac all the way through to Jacob and the Cherubic process by which the world must be restored to its original intent. This is where the process of restoration begins, making all of humanity into one body in the body that God created. The cherubic structure or cherubic body contains at least four faces and 24 wings (24 + 4 = 28 = 10). The cherubic principle is for manifesting new things. The cherubic activity is opening the doors for creation and manifestation, taking from the realm of ideas to the realm of actualization. The cherub functions in the ten realms in terms of being and relationality. It functions from the perspective of the twelve. Yet the number ten is important because we see God repeat it whenever the cherubic structure for manifesting creation is called for. It is not just the opening of gateways for things to come from another realm into this realm. It comes to the point of the cherubic structure creating something out of nothing. The number ten is vital. From what I discovered in the book of Ezekiel, the cherubim have 24 wings and with their four faces, we have 28, which is ten using simple gematria. Likewise, God gave Abram and Sarai five and five when He added the Hey to their names (Abraham and Sarah) because there was a creation coming or, if you will, a re-emergence of that which had disappeared from creation and its re-insertion into creation. Another way to look at this is from the perspective of Genesis 1. When God created, He spoke ten times and created the world. So, the cherubic function operates by ten, the binary. The cherubic relationality and interaction of being operates by way of twelve, which equals three (1+2=3). Three is the fundamental principle of interaction within Divinity. In terms of complete creation, it operates by way of 24, which is the number six, or 3 + 3. This allows for three above and three below which is six. The six illustrates the creation of man as a relational and relatable being who opens gates to manifest things that are already in creation to become manifest in a greater way in different dimensions. It is two different things.

We are not just dealing with the cherubic structure of the binary principle. I want you to know that the "1" and "0" or the principle of ten is present all the time. The cherubic structure contains the possibility of creating something out of nothing. Most cherubic structures are built as gateways for things that exist in other realms to transport them either into this realm or from this realm into another realm. But it can function in the construct of bringing that which does not yet exist into existence. I am not talking about bringing the invisible into visibility because the invisible can exist without being visible. I am talking about that which does not yet exist. So, when God creates out of nothing in the beginning, He frames the world. Even in that activity, you could still argue that God created the world out of things He had already made but we are using this word specifically to talk about bringing into creation something that did not exist before. This is what I meant when I referred back to Abraham and Sarah and bringing back into creation something that had disappeared out of creation. I am referring to the restoration of the cherubic structure that relates to the function of humanity as the co-creating agency with God.

This goes back to the relational principle of the self-existent God. In other words, the cherubic nature is also a way of relating to that which exists in the world to allow it to exchange spaces or inter-world places so that something that exists on the edge of the universe by the cherubic structure can be transported from one place to another and then manifested because of the interconnectivity within creation. Similarly, given the cherubic nature of the human being, we can push things back toward other dimensions or worlds as well. It is a bit of a philosophical distinction, but it is still there.

The thing about the principle of ten is that God is usually in charge of that kind of creation and then gives human beings permission to participate in it. When a human being's cherubic nature begins to come to the fore, then the human being begins to attract something that has been created that may be invisible in this realm but exists in other realms for manifesting it in this realm. The cherubic nature is an orientation towards the true God or, to use a cosmological term, the True North. The North Star is not always the same star. The people of the ancient world always knew that after some thousands of years, a new star takes over and the North Star becomes a different star. We have records from the Sumerians and Egyptians describing this phenomenon. Even the inhabitants of the Hindus Valley recorded the same thing.

As an aside, we know we live in space and we know that the Earth revolves around the sun, not the other way around. Yet we live our lives as if the sun revolves around the earth. So the way we live our lives is different from how things actually function and operate. Our language still talks about the rising and setting of the sun, yet we know that the sun does not rise and set. It makes for an easy life so people do not think you are crazy. The whole idea of the sun revolving around the Earth is a crazy idea because it is not true.

You may think that in Jacob the idea of idolatry is completely removed, yet you see Israel constantly running back to idolatry. By constantly reverting to idolatry, Israel corrupted its cherubic nature. God always told them that they were making that which was not a god into a god. In fact, at one point God says to Ephraim,

Ephraim is joined to idols;
leave him alone. (Hosea 4:17)

And again, God says,

Is Ephraim my dear son? Is he my darling child? (Jeremiah
31:20)

You see, as human beings we do not understand how objectifying our power or taking our power and putting it into an object diminishes us and how it messes up the possibility of our functioning as cherubic gateways for the movement of things. God created so many things that exist in these other worlds, but they are not here. God created some things, some technologies that are in creation. We do not know everything, but we do know of some things, yet we cannot bring them here. So we may continue to question whether we can create something new. Yes, we can because we have a cherubic nature. However, we do not have to create many of the things we seek; we just have to transport them. They already exist because our Father made sure of that. God created the Garden of Eden partly to give Adam a gateway for manifesting things in this realm that were already created. In the garden, God allowed Adam to manifest the animals into physical form in this creation. This means they came through a gate and that gate was both Adam and the garden. The manifestation happened through the arcing of the cherubic frequencies and resonance with the gate of the garden.

Do you know that the New Jerusalem has sound? It actually has a symphony—multiple sounds, one upon another. Do you remember the fugue that J. S. Bach was famous for (*Canon 3 a 2 per Motum contrarium* [*Ricercar Consort*])? He created this music that, as each level builds upon another level, it almost looks contrary to itself. In fact, it is sometimes called a *contrarium*. Yet at the end of the fugue, all the voices harmonize in an amazing way. These are the types of harmonic frequencies present in the cherubic nature of man and the cherubic gateway. The funny thing is that the cherubic gateway of the garden and Adam had the same DNA frequency so that when aligned with each other, they caused things to come from the other realm. I have referred to the fact that Eve is the one who manifested the serpent. The frequency that allowed the serpent to show itself is the same thing that the frequency of Cain's inner being did. It is something that now keeps the earth from manifesting certain things. God shut down those gateways because of Cain's sin. Consequently, you struggle to have things come to you. That which once came easily to you will no longer come precisely because you could not raise your brother from the dead. But God left that gateway, that cherubic structure in the life of Cain because he was forgiven. We know that Cain was of the evil one and committed evil, but then God forgive.

Now let us relate all of this towards Israel. The first thing God did with Jacob was to make him the gateway for the manifestation of the upper realm of heaven by having thirteen children—twelve sons and one daughter. All of them served as portals so God arranged them three by three by three by three, a triangular process that allows for influx. The center was a female womb because the center was a woman.

So the priesthood, as you have heard me teach, is a female function. Or you might say it is a "womb" function. This means that the womb is a crucible for framing cherubic natures. That is the reason why the watchers were trying to corrupt the female womb. It is the same reason the serpent wanted to corrupt Eve's womb. We can say the same thing in relation to Sarah. She knew that something was covering her and keeping her from conceiving. It did not hinder Abraham's fertility. So, Sarah created Hagar and made a separate cherubic structure that drew away the structure of idolatry. In other words, it turned the whole system that focuses on objects or clean systems into systems of worship. Now it does not mean that all unclean animals from scripture cannot be part of the cherubic structure. They can. However, they have to be purified to get to that point.

Let us relate this back to Jacob and his twelve children. If you notice, Dinah was not mentioned again after she was raped by Shechem the Hivite (Genesis 34). If she had not gone through that, the truth is that she should have been the priest. Think of it from this perspective. If Dinah was going to be a priest, she had to marry one of her brothers. I know your mind should have gone to what I am saying. You see, Abraham married his sister. There was a spiritual dimension in that union, but God began to cut incest off from Israel. It is part of the reason that Sarah could not completely cleanse the lineage until Jacob came. It is the same reason Isaac could not completely cleanse the lineage because it carried incest. God released Israel from incestuous relationships as a way of cleansing because incest is always accompanied by idolatry, witchcraft, and all the things that go with it. In fact, we can see the consequences of incest in the kings of Egypt. So, God purifies Israel from it. I think God had to remove Dinah because He had already spoken over Levi and told him he would not have an inheritance. In other words, it turned Levi into the feminine construct—not in the gay sense of the word, but rather as one who could open their being to dimensional or interstellar travel where things that exist in other realms can come through. The priest did not create these things, but he serves as the cherubic gateway by arcing with something other than himself that carries the same frequency. That is how the priest was able to bring things into this realm. And he is able to take things from this realm and throw it out of existence and into a world that does not exist.

Why does Jesus say this?

If you forgive the sins of any, they are forgiven them; if you withhold forgiveness from any, it is withheld. (John 20:23)

What makes this possible? You see, that is the point. The priest's cherubic structure and frequency arc with the same frequency in God. This frequency is in the foundation of creation that was before the foundation. When you arc yourself in this way you are able to remove something from this realm and put it out of existence completely. Forgiveness is the one priestly activity through which we remove sin completely from the world. In 2019, I preached a message where I said sin remains in the world because forgiveness is not present in the world. There is no true forgiveness in the world. Oh, please do not tell me you forgave someone because, if you did, that sin would cease to exist. We have not really learned. There is much more to this concept. Priesthood is a cherubic function, but prophecy is not. That is because priesthood removes sin; prophecy does not. If you seek prophecy, all it will do is reiterate your sin and your failure. It does not bring forgiveness because it is not cherubic in nature.

While we now have a cherubic priesthood, we must understand that it is much more than this idea of having a High Priest, because the High Priest was not the only priest in Israel. In fact, the High Priest had that role because all of Israel was combined to create the High Priest. The High Priest was a type of cherubic structure with twelve gateways sitting on his chest. The breastplate was a symbol of the twelve gateways of the lower part of the New Jerusalem, except it was structured for a cherubic being to wear. The ephod, which was the tunic that sat on the High Priest's shoulders, had the twelve names also. He had the upper realm on his shoulders because he was not the carrier of the upper realm. He was the carrier of the lower realm upon his heart. The ephod was just a reminder pointing to the possibility of the upper realm. The High Priest was a cherubic being, so much so, that there are stories of how his whole countenance, visage, and movements would change as he carried out his activities. Do you want to hear a strange story? It is said that the High Priest would manifest different faces of ancient Israelites as he walked toward the temple on the Day of Atonement. Remember, we have been talking a lot about the cherubic structure of the body. This is not what you refer to as necromancy, which is calling on the dead for magical purposes. In reality, as in the case of the High Priest, you should be relating to those who have died and are walking in the realm of the Father because of that cherubic interconnection. It is not necromancy if that person is alive and you are relating to them at a level of life that is not on this earth.

When Jacob had thirteen children, he created the possibility of a cherubic structure that serves as a gateway for things to come from that realm to this one. I will refer to invisible things, but by saying that they are invisible, I do not mean that they do not exist. Only modern scientific materialism will argue for the existence of things you do not see with the ordinary eye but still argues that anything that is not visible and cannot be detected by the five senses does not exist. The percentages of those who argue this way are a minority now. Yet there was a time when science only talked about things that you could see, taste, touch, hear, or smell. Now we know that many things exist that are difficult to capture with microscopes. For instance, we can see the effects of something, but we may not know what it is or what is causing a particular effect. No one argues anymore that invisible things do not exist. People used to say, "If I can't see it, it doesn't exist." No one says that anymore—not even the most materialistic scientists. In the priesthood, the cherubic structure serves as the thing that allows that which is invisible to become visible. It also allows for that which is created but not in your immediate domain to go from where it was created to here. It does not matter if it was created 300 billion light years away. Your cherubic structure will attract it to your vicinity when you tune your cherubic sound and being and arc it with that realm. You can do that. It is a matter of learning how to focus.

Before I ever knew that there are over 120 moons in our solar system, I had already started talking about how 120 is indicative of the end of the flesh. When I began to teach this concept, revelation started rushing towards me until one day it just landed. I was speaking with one of my students who heard me talk about the 120 and his research confirmed what I was saying. The cherubic structure I have been building along with the arcing with our moon and the moons of other planetary systems allowed me to bring the knowledge of that into this realm. I did the same thing when I began arcing with water. Throughout many ages, we have recognized that water is one of the most common substances, yet we do not know how to harness it. I have brought that knowledge of what was invisible into a knowledge in creation where it then can become manifest. It is a cherubic arcing.

Most human beings and even most believers have access to only one or two aspects of their cherubic nature. They do not even know what I am talking about when I refer to "cherubic nature." In fact, most human beings do not realize that they have more than three or four cherubic interactions occurring within their being. What if I say that you are a cherubic being and a human being on the earth, and your fundamental structure is 24? What if I push the envelope even further and say that when the angels were going up and down on Jacob's ladder, there were 24 angels from 24 different dimensions carrying 24 gateways up and down? Jacob is a human being from the earth. These numbers are always divisible by a certain number. The number of hours in a day is 24, which is divisible by six, the number of man. I just want to let you know that it is all about math. It is all about humanity. The fundamental structure that God gives us in creation is 24, which then serves upon new structures that are built. Even other structures that have been built before arc based on how the earth affects other places. I continue to say that the earth is the headquarters of God's universe. That is what the Bible teaches us.

> **And God said, "Let the earth sprout vegetation, plants yielding seed, and fruit trees bearing fruit in which is their seed, each according to its kind, on the earth." And it was so. The earth brought forth vegetation, plants yielding seed according to their own kinds, and trees bearing fruit in which is their seed, each according to its kind. And God saw that it was good. (Genesis 1:11-12)**

His word is not "Let the heavens bring forth." He said, "Let the earth. . ." and the atmosphere responded. You may want to call that the "heavens," but in Hebrew it is just the sky and the environment of the earth. The environment of the earth is the crucible for creation because of its cherubic nature. It is the prototypical cherubic structure that all of the planetary systems of the universe must mimic in order to produce life. They will tailor themselves after the earth.

The people of Israel in the wilderness, symbolically and metaphorically, represented the cherubic gateways. Their worship in the wilderness and their movement was supposed to arc with other cherubic structures. Let us take that one step further. The whole of Israel comprised the cherubic priesthood and embodied the cherubic nature in one person known as the High Priest who carried all of them on his heart. So, while the outward movement of the cherubic structures was reflected in the movement of the twelve tribes of Israel, the priests reflected the cherubic structures' embodiment. In this way, the twelve tribes are transformed into the gateways that became a part of his being. It is a mystery. All the sacrifices of Israel to open dimensions and portals must go through the High Priest. On the Day of Atonement, all of these gateways converge upon the High Priest. So, he opens a gateway for the cleansing and renewing of Israel. All the things God created on the fifth day were cherubic in nature and they framed the context for bringing things or removing things. All the animals used for Israeli sacrifices were created on the fifth day. Especially for the Day of Atonement, the goat had become the carrier of Israel's sin into the wilderness. But, again, this was because every animal that God created on the fifth day was cherubic in nature. The clean animals especially, as God defined them, had the capacity to open up gateways. Animals cannot open gateways as well as humanity does. However, when man fell, the cherubic gateways of the animal kingdom became purer than humanity. For that reason, they could open much more effective gateways until humanity was restored.

So, Israel became one being. You can look at them as a family or you can look at the High Priest as the embodiment of Israel. The entire garment of the High Priest is a revelation of where God is going with the cherubic nature. God built Jacob or Israel to be a cherubic structure to receive from different dimensions. Israel can access everything on this earth created by God because they are one of the few nations who actually build themselves up in this context. Now they are no longer there, but that cherubic structure remains in the consciousness of the Jew. The organization in the wilderness was to allow them to bring towards them whatever has been created, no matter in what realm it resides. We know that the Egyptians gave them gold because they were supposed to give them a wage, but the question is how much gold. When you read about how much gold it took to build the Ark of the Covenant and all the other components, there is no way Israel brought all that gold from Egypt. Remember, Israel is a cherubic being and the cherubic structure is not just organic. It is metal-based and stone-based (precious stones) as well. That is why the breastplate is a cherubic structure because it had all of the living stones on it. All of the stones had different frequencies that became one in the process of seeking the face of the Lord. They harmonized. The ephod harmonized by "yes" and "no." The stones on the breastplate were harmonized by the movement of their frequencies. This allowed the orchestration of stones so that they had the sounds created by God that were balanced and harmonized. After the High Priest went into the Tabernacle and came out again, his whole body became musical and the frequency of his being was heard throughout Israel. This signified an alignment in which the sound of God's creative voice and forgiveness resounded for Israel. The people then responded with their own sound.

Let us talk about Moses. Moses is, as far as we know, the only human being who physically became a cherub. He is the one God used to structure Israel. What did God do with Moses? I am going to tell you biblical stories that will help you see from a different perspective. Moses, after he killed the Egyptian and left Egypt, began walking with a staff. It is a common African tradition. I know you do not want to think of Moses as African—you think he is Charleton Heston. But Moses was an African. In any case, it is a common thing for African kings and elders to walk with a staff. It is our culture. In those days, an elder who walked without a staff was not considered to be walking rightly. It is not for leaning or killing snakes. It is a symbol of authority and a key for opening things up.

When he was in the wilderness, Moses saw a burning bush. What if the burning bush was the embodiment of the nature of Moses, but he was unaware of that fact? Remember that Moses was an African and an Egyptian. That kind of experience was not normal. Moses was a magician in the house of Pharaoh. Do not forget that, even though he was born by a Hebrew woman, he was an African chief's son. Let us call it what it was—Pharaoh was an African chief. That was before the Arabs took over Africa and before the Visigoths and Ostrogoths took over when North Africa was all black people. It was before they moved and were attacked, and the move stopped. I say that to you so that you will understand what it means when we say someone is a chief's child. If you are Native American, you can clearly understand this. You are taught all kinds of things that are specific to your particular culture. Someone who comes from that background understands this.

Moses, being from this culture, had been trained in understanding the mysteries (Acts 7:22). He was actually involved in Egyptian magic and African rituals. Many of the miracles he did were based on that worldview. We like to pass over that passage. But we need to see that

Moses was a practitioner. That is exactly why God chose him. If he were just an academic, he would not have been able to do anything. In fact, you could not be an academic in Egypt without being someone who was initiated into the mysteries. His first cherubic encounter was looking at a tree, which is also a human being. But he could not be some other tree. It had to be the tree that is Moses, burning but not being destroyed. He encountered his own angelic self, talking, not just burning. And God speaks through the fire. This is what I just said. It is a cherubic frequency. Moses turns his intention to the tree, God speaks, and there is an arcing within that context. Now God can speak from the other realm to Moses. But without activating the cherubic structure of Moses' being, Moses would never have been able to hear God or be able to experience Him. This means that the cherubic nature is something that amplifies or opens up the soundwaves of Divinity and amplifies it so that the human being can hear it.

God spoke to Moses and the staff turned into a serpent. Moses picked it up and it changed.

> **The LORD said to him, "What is that in your hand?" He said, "A staff." And he said, "Throw it on the ground." So he threw it on the ground, and it became a serpent, and Moses ran from it. But the LORD said to Moses, "Put out your hand and catch it by the tail"—so he put out his hand and caught it, and it became a staff in his hand. . . . (Exodus 4:2-4)**

And God called it the staff of Moses, but when Moses went up, he called it the staff of God.

> **And Moses took the staff of God in his hand. (Exodus 4:20).**

We tend to ignore that passage. When the staff became a snake, it is not just some ordinary magic. Like everything else that God does, when one becomes a cherubic being, everything that God gives that person draws from that cherubic structure. Thus, the staff that Moses walked with is called the staff of God at a certain point.

You need to study some of the Jewish texts to understand why Pharaoh was so afraid of Moses. Why was he? Pharaoh was a god who could manifest himself as other beings like a jackal, hawk, or eagle. Yet when Moses came before him, Pharaoh was afraid of Moses. Why did Pharaoh not kill Moses from the beginning? Well, you could say that

God protected him, but even at this point, God used Moses' cherubic nature to protect him. How do I know that? Because when Moses finally went into the presence of God and came back, his face grew horns:

And when Moses came down from the mount Sinai, he held the two tables of the testimony, and he knew not that his face was horned from the conversation of the Lord. (Exodus 34:29 [Douay-Rheims Bible])

This means that, if Pharaoh was who he was supposed to be, he already saw that in Moses before Moses ever saw it in himself. Remember, these guys who are not believers, such as the Egyptians and Hindus, respect their gods. They would not kill their gods. So, if Moses is revealing a cherubic structure, the Pharaoh would not kill him. Moses may have not yet been aware of his cherubic nature, but he knew as an Egyptian that he could become any kind of creature he wanted to be. When Moses' true cherubic nature was revealed and horns appeared on his face, the Bible says that he did not know that he had grown horns on his face, like a bull. So, they had to cover his face until the horns when back inside, but when they did, he refused to remove the veil because he did not want the people to know that they had receded back into his body. This is why Paul said the veil was upon the Israelites every time the law was read (2 Corinthians 3:14) because the law was read under the cherubic structure. However, when the cherubic glory was dissipating, Moses did not remove the veil so they were still thinking about the law under the one dimension of the cherub.

Since we have such a hope, we are very bold, not like Moses, who would put a veil over his face so that the Israelites might not gaze at the outcome of what was being brought to an end. But their minds were hardened. For to this day, when they read the old covenant, that same veil remains unlifted, because only through Christ is it taken away. Yes, to this day whenever Moses is read a veil lies over their hearts. (2 Corinthians 3:12-15)

So, Moses had this experience with God that allowed this aspect of his being to be revealed. In reality, Moses had a four-sided face, but the Israelites could only see one. The reason they could only see one side is that at the time of Moses' manifestation of the faces, the bull was reigning in the sky (Taurus). This is one reason the Israelites tried to create the golden calf. God also revealed the bull in the structure of Moses' cherubic being to keep them from idol worship, to show them that the real thing they were seeking was actually already a part of them as human beings. It is Israel. You do not transfer your being to an object! Oh, come on. You have just seen Moses grow horns!

I do not think that the Bible is written in linear form. Some rabbis have said Moses changed after the golden calf. Even so, God told Israel that the idol they built is not something into which they want to project their cherubic nature. This nature is inside of them, not outside. It applies to us as well. Stop projecting into something else. It has to be human.

 The same structure is around the High Priest. What you do not see in the High Priestly crown is the Shin Gadol, which has four horns. It is like a Shin, but it has four horns, not three. If you were looking at the Shin Gadol from a Native American perspective, you would see someone wearing antlers. One of the things we forget as modern Christians is that the ancient people did have understanding and revelation of things in heaven, but they did not have the technology to make it look good. They just took animal horns and put it on their heads. All of our ancestors did that. We should stop thinking that they were stupid. Sometimes they saw heavenly sacrifice and things moving in the heavenly realms, but instead of finding the reality, they killed their fellow human beings and poured their blood on the altars to access these mysteries.

So, Moses came down from heaven and met with Bezalel and the people of Israel:

> **Then Moses said to the people of Israel, "See, the LORD has called by name Bezalel the son of Uri, son of Hur, of the tribe of Judah; and he has filled him with the Spirit of God, with skill, with intelligence, with knowledge, and with all craftsmanship, to devise artistic designs, to work in gold and silver and bronze, in cutting stones for setting, and in carving wood, for work in every skilled craft." (Exodus 35:30-33)**

Bezalel used the letters that God used to create the world. When God gave Abraham and Sarah the Hey (when He changed their names from Abram and Sarai), He reactivated the language by which He created the universe in the DNA of Abraham. That is how Hebrew became the language of the earth. So, in the case of Bezalel, the Hebrew letters are cherubic letters. They are used to frame the cherubic body. Bezalel was able to use the letters to create all the parts of the tabernacle. In turn, all the parts of the tabernacle are a reflection of the human body at a certain level. I am not just talking about the three sections but also about the various things that are in it. He prepares each part of the tabernacle and uses the cherubic letters to create the tabernacle as a cherubic body, a living thing. He created all these parts (we like to say 613, but there were more) and all the parts sat alone. Moses, being a cherubic being, now has to arc his voice with the cherubic structures of heaven. I once taught about the ten names of God that Moses used to lift up the ark. The Bible does not say that Israel put all of the pieces together. It says Moses "raised the tabernacle."

And it came to pass in the first month of the second year, on the first day of the month, that the tabernacle was raised up. So Moses raised up the tabernacle, fastened its sockets, set up its boards, put in its bars, and raised up its pillars. (Exodus 40:17-18 [NKJ])

He caused the tabernacle to stand. This is the same word (וַיָּקֶם or vai-ya-kem) we see in Isaiah when God says,

Arise, shine, for your light has come and the glory of the LORD has risen upon you. (Isaiah 60:1)

Moses could not have raised the tabernacle and caused the infusion of the energetic structure of Divinity if his own cherubic nature was not on this plane. When the tabernacle was built, the Ark of the Covenant was also made. All the components were all made together. And what was placed on the Ark? Two cherubs whose wings arced with each other were situated on top of the Ark.

I want to talk about the cherubic gateway and what happens where those wings meet and where the sound of the High Priest and of Israel arced with the sound from the point of the creation of the world. We will figure this out and end up talking about who the Bible says we are, and why we are struggling with all of this. I will tell you that Jesus is not coming tomorrow and I will keep telling you that because we are not yet manifesting our cherubic nature.

The cherubic structure makes it possible for ordinary things to become an attraction for what God made in heaven to come to earth. If no complete cherubic being is present, those things stay on the other side. It means the gateways are not aligned. Even the flow of divine power, might, wisdom and understanding comes only when there is a cherubic being who is aware of who they are and begins to arc their voice with the sound that is coming from the tabernacle on the other side. When that happens, if you listen to some of our worship times, you can hear the arcing process going on because it changes the atmosphere. No one has to tell you it is happening. It happens by the arcing of the voices of the cherub, which is the voice of tongues. It is amazing to me that Pentecostals do not understand this. I often have to pull teeth in church to get people to speak in tongues. Why would I have to force you to speak in tongues? This is your arcing with the dimensions of heaven to open up cherubic gateways for the manifestation of things from that realm to this realm! So why must I force you? You can remain blind and locked up if you want. I do not argue with churches about this anymore. I will just go to a place and start speaking in tongues for about twenty minutes. The crazy religious Christians start getting upset and fidgety because the force in them starts saying, "I don't want to be here. I don't want to be here." But I do it anyway and the offense keeps rising until it breaks. Then when the concert of voices comes, there is an arcing between here and there.

To summarize, Moses raised the tabernacle. The parts were made and imbued with the cherubic alphabet, which was used for mixing and creating the world. God reactivated the letters through Abraham in Israel. Now, through Moses, God used that very structure to create a miniature of the worlds. He allowed the cherubic structure to be the basis for framing and raising of the tabernacle in the wilderness. It became the principle for activating the Ark. Without the activation of the human cherub, the Ark remains just an object. In the same way, as long as the church does not understand its cherubic nature, the world will remain untransformed. We continue in our immaturity without understanding who we truly are. Somehow, we think screaming and doing some spiritual mumbo jumbo without operating from our cherubic nature is going to be effective. Do not be presumptuous, but you must walk from that perspective of knowing who you are. Moses did that. Once the Ark of the Covenant had been activated, Israel's whole life changed in the wilderness.

I want to show you something. Did you ever wonder why Israel met the people in Canaan? When the spies came back, they said they looked like grasshoppers. They did not understand that looking like grasshoppers was the real intent. God wanted them to look like grasshoppers because grasshoppers are cherubic beings. Some grasshoppers have eight wings; some have six. They are cherubic creatures. So, when you read the Hebrew word for grasshopper, you realize that this was a way for them to actually see themselves as cherubs! But they did not see it. They took it as a negative sign and reacted accordingly. Do you remember that I told you that you have never seen anything in nature in its intended form? You see the diminished forms of what these creatures looked like before man fell. If you were walking down the road and you saw a creatures with four faces—a dog face, a cat face, a fish face, a bird face—you would not believe that God sent it. As much as you love dogs or cats, you would not believe God sent it. If you were to actually see a cherub the way Ezekiel saw it, you have to have a framework for saying, "This is God." The problem these spies had was they forgot what they had seen in the wilderness as they were operating in the heavenly dimensions for the three or four years before then. They walked around these realms. They saw Moses become a cherub. They saw how the tabernacle was built. Yet when they saw themselves as grasshoppers, they did not see themselves in terms of the grasshopper's real nature in its cherubic structure; they saw themselves in its diminished construct. Preachers are right when they say that they did not look at themselves with eyes of faith. This is powerful.

What does God say about the locusts? He says, "My army" (Joel 2).

The word of the LORD that came to Joel, the son of Pethuel:
An Invasion of Locusts
Hear this, you elders;
give ear, all inhabitants of the land!
Has such a thing happened in your days,
or in the days of your fathers?
Tell your children of it,
and let your children tell their children,
and their children to another generation.
What the cutting locust left,

the swarming locust has eaten.
What the swarming locust left,
the hopping locust has eaten,
and what the hopping locust left,
the destroying locust has eaten. (Joel 1:1-4)

If you just read it from the literal perspective, it sounds like the locusts are just doing what locusts do, but the truth is all of these things are diminished beings of the cherubic structures of creation. Now they are so low because, if they were in their original nature, they would be ruling us, not us ruling them. You have never really seen an elephant or a lion in its actual nature. You even know what an elephant looks like in this realm, but an elephant is diminished. As big as it is, it is not in its original construct. Everything in creation has been diminished, brought low, and subdued by God so that you can rule. They will remain that way until you develop your cherubic nature, until you are aware of who you are in terms of your multidimensional being.

Are you a member of the body of Christ? If the body of Christ is a cherubic body, then you have access to billions and billions of people and energies and structures because you are a part of that cherubic body. Part of cherubic power is having access to other technologies that may not be inherent in you or maybe low in you but you can tie yourself to others who have it. We are members of one another.

We who are strong have an obligation to bear with the failings
of the weak, and not to please ourselves.
(Romans 15:1)

We tend to look at this as morality. For instance, we think if someone is lying, then someone should help them stop lying. But this passage refers to more than that. This is so important because you are a part of that cherubic body where you have connection to people who have lived thousands of years before you. And you have connection to the crazy African woman who is praying underneath that tree in Timbuktu. And she has access to you.

All of this is about you. Who do you think you are as it relates to this cherubic structure? You have seen that you carry cherubic gateways and that by arcing your voice with the voice of the body of Christ and with the voice from heaven, you can actually open up dimensions where things that have been created there can become visible here.

COMMUNION ACTIVATION:

Let us do communion together. We want to take this communion as a way of affirming our powers as priests for the transmutation of creation.

Type the following web address into your browser to participate in communion with Dr. Ogbonnaya and affirm our priesthood:

https://www.aactev8.com/course?courseid=aactev8-media-archives

Then select **Chapter 5 Communion**. You will need to sign in to your free Aactev8 account.

Communion Transcription

Take the bread. This is my body given for you. Take and eat in remembrance of me.

This cup is the new covenant in my blood. Take and drink all of it and, as you do, remember me. Lord Jesus Christ, your body and your blood, the body and the blood, the body and the blood. Blessed are You, O Lord our God, King of the Universe. Give us the bread from heaven. You gave your Son who poured out His life as a drink offering. Give us the privilege of drinking from His life and the light of His being. We worship You, Father. You are holy and majestic. We sing your praise and magnify your Name. With all the angels and the archangels, with all the Ophanim and Erelim, with all who bless your Name above, with all the crown-wearing elders, Father, and the surrounding beings, with all those who have gone before, with all the men and women in white linen who give You glory, my God and my King, who constantly behold your face, with all the angelic structures, we honor You. And we join them and we say, holy, holy, holy is the Lord God of Hosts. Behold the whole earth is filled with your glory. We speak to You, Lamb of God. You are worthy to receive glory, honor, power, and victory because it is You who has redeemed us and by your blood, You have made us kings and priests, even priests to God, our Father. And to You who sits upon the throne, O Father, and to the Lamb, blessings and honor, glory, wisdom forever and ever. Hallelujah! His kingdom and His tabernacle are with us.

The body of Christ. The cup of the new covenant, the blood of Jesus.

This is symbolic. Bring the bread from heaven down. Take it to your right. Take it to your left. Bring it to the center. Wait, wait. Take it up again. Gently bring it down. Hold it bring it to a center take it from the center. Pick it up. Take it to the right. Take it down. Take it to the left. Bring it to the center. Take it from the center, take it up. Take it to the left. Take it down. Take it to the right. Bring it to the center. Make a circle about it in the center.

With all the Angels and the Archangels, with all the Crown Ones, Keterim with all the Ophanim, with all the Arelim, with all the Seraphim with all the Hashmalim, with all the Melechim, with all the Beni-Elohim.

With all the Tarshashim, with all the Paninim, Daminim, with all, with all, with all. With all those who hold the foundations and all the righteous who are the foundations of worlds, with all the Cherubim... we raise the bread.

Eyeh Asher Eyeh, YHVH, Elohim, EL, YA, YHVH-Adonai, Elohim-Zavaot, Yahweh-Zavaot, El Shaddai, Adonai Kol Ha Eretz, and the Name above all names Yeshua Hamashiach.

At the Name of Jesus Christ every knee bows, every tongue confesses in heaven, on earth, underneath the earth, in all creation. Lord, your body was given for us. And now with great thanksgiving Father, by Your Name Yeshua, by Your commandment, we transmute this to your body and this to your blood, Bread from Heaven... Drink from Eden... the body of Christ, Father for the healing of our body, for the tuning of our body, for the tuning of our soul.

Thank You Lord Jesus. "This is my body, take, eat".

Blood of Jesus, the blood of Jesus, the life of the Son of God. Worthy are You, oh Lamb of God, Who by Your blood has redeemed us and has made us Kings and Priests to God, our Father.

The blood of Jesus, the blood of our Lord Jesus Christ.

ABOUT THE AUTHOR

Adonijah Okechukwu Ogbonnaya (BA, MATS, MA, Ph.D.) is the founder of AACTEV8 International, an Apostolic, and Kingdom Ministry which works with the Body of Christ across the globe for Soul Winning, Discipleship, Training, and Equipping the saints in Kingdom mysteries and Kingdom living. Located in Venice, California, Dr. Ogbonnaya (also known as A. Okechukwu or "Dr. O") has focused on helping believers engage the spiritual realities that have been opened up for them in the person of the Lord Jesus Christ. He is a Hebrew-born native of Nigeria, West Africa. He earned his Ph.D. and Master's degree in theology and personality and his Master's in religion from Claremont School of Theology. He completed his M.A. in theological studies at Western Evangelical Seminary and his B.A. in religion at Hillcrest Christian College in Canada. He also holds a Ph.D. in business publishing.

He is the presenter of numerous teachings found at: www.aactev8.com.

Dr. Ogbonnaya is married to Pastor Benedicta and is blessed with four wonderful children and grandchildren.

SeraphCreative

Heaven's Heart for Earth

Seraph Creative is a collective of artists, writers, theologians & illustrators who desire to see the body of Christ grow into full maturity, walking in their inheritance as Sons Of God on the Earth.

Sign up to our newsletter to know about the release of the next book in the series, as well as other exciting releases.

Visit our website : www.seraphcreative.org